Prince Edward County, Virginia School Closing

Dr. Terence Hicks and his colleagues have provided us with an important historiography surrounding the landmark Prince Edward County School closing. This edited volume offers deep personal insights about the fierce resistance to school segregation, as we strategize and formulate current solutions to make our public schools more equitable today. This book is a must-read for anyone concerned about educational equity.

—*Jamal Watson, PhD*, **Executive Editor,**
Diverse: Issues in Higher Education,
Professor, Trinity Washington University

The current political assault on truth heightens the necessity of researchers, historians, and educational leaders in particular to produce and support accurate historial accounts. In that respect, more can be learned and extrapolated from additional scholarship surrounding school closures in Prince Edward County, Virginia in the wake of Brown v. Board of Education. The work of Terence Hicks and associates on this topic is greatly needed!

—*Jasmine Williams, PhD*, **San Francisco State University**

Prince Edward County, Virginia School Closing

A Compilation of Research Studies

Edited by

Terence Hicks
East Tennessee State University, USA

United Kingdom – North America – Japan
India – Malaysia – China

Emerald Publishing Limited
Emerald Publishing, Floor 5, Northspring, 21-23 Wellington Street, Leeds LS1 4DL

First edition 2025

Copyright © 2025 by Emerald Publishing Limited.
All rights of reproduction in any form reserved.

Cover photo: Prince Edward marches for freedom: 1963. Photo by Thomas J. O'Halloran. The image is courtesy of the Library of Congress, reproduction number LC-DIG-ppmsca-37257 (digital file from original).

Reprints and permissions service
Contact: www.copyright.com

No part of this book may be reproduced, stored in a retrieval system, transmitted in any form or by any means electronic, mechanical, photocopying, recording or otherwise without either the prior written permission of the publisher or a licence permitting restricted copying issued in the UK by The Copyright Licensing Agency and in the USA by The Copyright Clearance Center. Any opinions expressed in the chapters are those of the authors. Whilst Emerald makes every effort to ensure the quality and accuracy of its content, Emerald makes no representation implied or otherwise, as to the chapters' suitability and application and disclaims any warranties, express or implied, to their use.

British Library Cataloguing in Publication Data
A catalogue record for this book is available from the British Library

ISBN: 978-1-83708-909-3 (Print hardback)
ISBN: 978-1-83708-911-6 (Print paperback)
ISBN: 978-1-83708-908-6 (Ebook)
ISBN: 978-1-83708-910-9 (Epub)

Typeset by TNQ Tech
Index created by Illumindexing, Freelance Editing/Indexing Services

CONTENTS

About the Editor .... *vii*

About the Contributors .... *ix*

Foreword .... *xiii*

Acknowledgments .... *xv*

Introduction .... *xvii*

1. The Potential of Government-Sponsored Restorative Justice: A US Case Study of the *Brown* Scholarship Fund *1*
   Linda J. Mann

2. Prince Edward County's Role in *Brown v. Board of Education* and the Birth of Massive Resistance *21*
   Emily Martin Cochran

3. Remembering the Past, Looking Toward the Future: The Role of Memory and Racial Healing in the Preservation of R. R. Moton High *49*
   Dwana Waugh

4. The Power of the Primary Source: Using a Case Study of Prince Edward County, Virginia (1951–1964) to Teach the Civil Rights Movement *71*
   Caitlin B. Maloney

5. A Case Study of Black Students' Education and Socialization Since Public School Closure in Prince Edward County, Virginia 89
Jeffrey Carlton Scales

6. Addressing Silence: Oral History as a Tool to Teach Difficult History... 111
Rory Dunn

7. School Has a "Place" ... Every Place Except Farmville, Prince Edward County, Virginia 129
Alicia Pennington

Index.. *143*

ABOUT THE EDITOR

Dr. Terence Hicks has served as an academic Dean for the Clemmer College of Education at East Tennessee State University and the Whitlowe R. Green College of Education at Prairie View A&M University, Texas, a member of the Texas A&M University System. Most recently, he has served as a Distinguished Visiting Professor for the Southern Regional Education Board (SREB), headquartered in Atlanta, Georgia and as a Research Fellow for the National Institutes of Health, National Center of Minority Health and Health Disparities. Currently, Dr. Hicks is serving as a tenured full professor in the Department of Educational Leadership and Policy Analysis at East Tennessee State University in Johnson City, Tennessee.

Dr. Hicks is a 2024 Legacy Award recipient, an accomplished award-winning author, an award-winning university academic Dean, and an award-winning Social Scientist. As a Social Scientist, he is a cited authority in the area of the first generation college student population and has presented academic papers both nationally/internationally. He has been cited across all seven continents, and received high visibility in countries such as South Africa, China, Germany, Mexico, India, Philippines, Indonesia, Thailand, and the United States. To date, he has published eleven (11) books in the field of higher education/college student population and over 100 combined research publications and/or presentations. Most recently, his book titled "*An Educational Journey to Deanship: A Memoir*" won the 2021 Living Now Book Award in the *memoir category*. Additionally, he has been interviewed and cited in Diverse Issues in Higher Education, USA Today, Research Alert National Yearbook, Detroit News, ABC-KTKA Channel 49 in Topeka, Kansas, KPVU-FM 91.3 (Texas) Public Affairs talk show, WFSS 91.9 FM (North Carolina), Fayetteville Observer, Journal of Blacks in Higher Education, Johnson City Press and many university websites, peer-reviewed journals and books.

Dr. Hicks holds a bachelor and master degree from Virginia State University, a doctorate in Education degree from Wilmington University, Delaware and a Ph.D. from North Carolina State University. Also, he is the President of Hicks Research Consulting, LLC, a comprehensive consulting company that provide research evaluation/assessment for universities, school districts, community colleges and community agencies.

ABOUT THE CONTRIBUTORS

Emily Martin Cochran holds an MA in public history and a Ph.D. in history from the University of South Carolina. Dr. Cochran is currently the historic resources survey coordinator with the Georgia Historic Preservation Division. She is a native of Clover, Virginia, and currently lives in Rome, Georgia, with her family.

Rory Dunn is a doctoral student at Virginia Commonwealth University. His research interests pertain to the complexities of rural identity and the interaction between rural identity and classroom instruction, as well as critical historical inquiry practices. Currently, he works with preservice social studies teachers in developing their historical thinking practices at Randolph-Macon College and VCU. In addition to his work in education, he is passionate about history. He has conducted oral history projects in Prince Edward County, Virginia, and is currently working on an oral history project about the historically Black neighborhood of North Barton Heights in Richmond, Virginia.

Caitlin B. Maloney graduated with a BA in history from Radford University in 2018, where she won the Winesett Awards for Library Research for her history capstone project titled "Through the Perilous Fight: The National Anthem, the Stars and Stripes, and American Sports." After graduating, she became a high school history teacher and won the Veterans of Foreign Wars National Citizenship Education Award from her local VFW chapter. In 2020, she began her MA coursework in public history at Southern New Hampshire University and graduated in 2022 with her capstone, "A Microhistory of Prince Edward County, Virginia, 1951–1963: Civil Rights Curriculum for Virginia's Secondary Educators," published in ProQuest. She is currently a college navigator and adjunct history instructor. Outside of academic and work pursuits, she enjoys traveling and spending time with her husband and three dogs: Appa, Cooper, and Rollo.

Linda J. Mann is a leading director and researcher on racial redress initiatives at the intersection of US history, international human rights, and racial repair. She has written widely about local and state reparative justice, descendant engagement, and justice potentials and is the cofounder of the African American Redress Network. Dr. Mann is executive director at the John Mitchell Jr. Project at George Mason's Carter School for Peace and Reconciliation and is also an assistant adjunct professor at Columbia University's School of International and Public Affairs. Previously, she served as executive director at the Civil Rights and Restorative Justice Project, Northeastern University, and as vice president of research for the Georgetown Memory Project.

Alicia Pennington is an independent scholar in urban education with an emphasis on the importance of "place" in the education lives of African Americans. Her research interests include how Black women navigate housing, education, and transportation issues in the acquisition of educational opportunities. She has a Ph.D. from Temple University and over 15 years of teaching experience.

Jeffrey Carlton Scales is a native of Cumberland, Virginia, and has over 19 years as a secondary school administrator and over 27 years total in secondary and adult education. He has served throughout his career as a teacher in elementary, middle, and high schools; an assistant principal of high schools; a principal of elementary and high schools; and a director for a central office all in central Virginia. Currently, he is in his third year as a regional principal with the Virginia Department of Corrections—Correctional Education. Dr. Scales completed his doctorate from Liberty University in educational leadership. His dissertation was a case study that researched the 5-year closure of Prince Edward County Public School (1959–1964) and its impact on the education and socialization of African American students there over 50 years later. He finished his master's degree from Virginia State University in educational administration and supervision and his bachelor's degree from James Madison University in political science.

Dwana Waugh is an associate professor of history at Sweet Briar College. She received her B.A. in history and education from Randolph-Macon Woman's College and earned her M.A. and Ph.D. in American history from the University of North Carolina at Chapel Hill. Her research focuses on African American educational history, especially public and oral histories. She examines the connections between race, politics, and historical memory in southern education. Her current research project investigates the complicated and complex legacies of school desegregation in Prince

Edward County, Virginia, as the county shifted from massive resistance to massive reconciliation. As a former public high school teacher, she is committed to exploring these connections between the contemporary past with recent educational policies. Dr. Waugh teaches courses in US history, African American history, historical memory, and educational methodology.

FOREWORD

In Dr. Terence Hicks's insightful exploration, the narrative of Prince Edward County, Virginia, unfolds, revealing a critical period when public schools were closed to resist desegregation. This act of educational deprivation against African Americans is a stark reminder of systemic racism's depth and the enduring fight for equality. My journey, intersecting with the Civil Rights Movement alongside Dr. Martin Luther King Jr. and in academia, underscores my belief in education's transformative power for societal justice.

Dr. Hicks's comprehensive research provides a window into the struggles, resilience, and activism that characterized the response to the Prince Edward County school closures. This historical episode serves as a backdrop for understanding the broader fight against racial injustice and the pivotal role of education as a vehicle for change. This book intricately details the community's battle for their children's right to education and the subsequent initiatives for restorative justice, such as the Brown Scholarship Fund, highlighting the importance of confronting our past to mend the fabric of our society.

Through this volume, Dr. Hicks invites readers to reflect on the complexities of racial equality and the ongoing efforts required to achieve it. His work not only pays homage to those who fought tirelessly for their rights but also offers a blueprint for future generations to continue this crucial work. As we delve into these pages, let us draw inspiration from the past and commit to the path of education, understanding, and action toward a more just and equitable world. This book is a testament to the power of resilience and the imperative of education in our collective journey toward justice. It challenges us to reflect on our contributions to this ongoing struggle and to recognize education's role as a fundamental right and a cornerstone of democracy.

Robert L. Green, PhD
Civil Rights Pioneer
Former President, University of the District of Columbia
Dean and Professor Emeritus
Urban Affairs Program, Michigan State University

ACKNOWLEDGMENTS

I would like to thank the production and marketing staff at Information Age Publishing and Emerald Publishing for endorsing and assisting with this book on the Prince Edward County, Virginia, school closure. I am also appreciative for the editing assistance of Tricia Currie-Knight.

INTRODUCTION

Terence Hicks

Brown v. Board of Education of Topeka, the landmark 1954 Supreme Court case in which the justices ruled unanimously that the racial segregation of children in public schools was unconstitutional, turns 70 years old this year. As one of the five civil rights cases that were combined in *Brown*, the *Davis v. County School Board of Prince Edward County* case was instrumental, as it challenged the segregation of students in public schools.

> Rather than desegregate, on June 26, 1959, the Prince Edward County Board of Supervisors refused to appropriate money from the county school board to the public schools. This refusal, which continued for five years, was part of the Massive Resistance Movement, a state government policy to block the desegregation of public schools, which effectively closed the doors of the county's schools (Zinn Education Project).

During the 5-year closure of the Prince Edward County schools, there were many community and student protests. On March 28, 1962, Dr. Martin Luther King Jr. visited Prince Edward County and led a protest rally with students and community leaders at a local Baptist church. After the Supreme Court ordered the reopening of Prince Edward County schools, US attorney general Robert F. Kennedy would also visit Prince Edward County on May 11, 1964, to observe the Free Schools. And as seen on the cover of this book, it has been over 60 years since residents from Prince Edward County, Virginia, were part of the crowd that participated in the August 28, 1963, march on Washington for jobs and freedom.

I too am a native of Prince Edward County, Virginia, and a direct descendant of the Prince Edward County (1959–1964) school lockout. My parents were among 1,700 African American students who were forced to cope with the absence of public schooling in Prince Edward County.

xviii *Introduction*

In 2010, I co-edited a book alongside Abul Pitre titled *The Educational Lockout of African Americans in Prince Edward County, Virginia (1959–1964): Personal Accounts and Reflections*. This book provided interesting findings on Grassroots schools, the Kennedy administration, an African American movement during the Prince Edward County school closings, and personal reflections and a lecture from four professors whose parents were affected by the Prince Edward County lockout. Similar to *The Educational Lockout of African Americans in Prince Edward County, Virginia (1959–1964)*, this book—The *Prince Edward County, Virginia School Closing: A Compilation of Research Studies*—provides readers with a series of qualitative methodology approaches and topics surrounding the Prince Edward County School closing as it relates to educational crizes, social class, race, Black determination, Black education, White resistance, massive resistance, and educational struggles.

This edited volume highlights a group of dynamic contributors and a foreword written by a civil rights pioneer. In my memoir, *An Educational Journey to Deanship* (2021), I wrote about influential African Americans who were affiliated with Prince Edward County, Virginia: most notably, Dr. Robert Russa Moton, Dr. Mary Elizabeth Branch, Dr. James West, and Reverend Francis Griffin. In addition to Moton, Branch, West, and Griffin, there were other noted prominent leaders who were not natives of Prince Edward County but were known for their work within the county, like Dr. William Edward Burghardt Du Bois and Dr. Robert L. Green.

Dr. BuDois was probably the most influential African American of the 20th century. In July and August of 1897, he spent time in Prince Edward County, Virginia, to complete a rural case study titled "The Negroes of Farmville, Virginia" for the Department of Labor. Dr. Robert L. Green, who wrote the foreword for this book, lived in Prince Edward County, Virginia, for a short period of time. Dr. Green is a renowned researcher, former president of the University of the District of Columbia, and former dean of the College of Urban Development at Michigan State University. From 1965 through 1967, he worked for Dr. Martin Luther King Jr. as the education director of the Southern Christian Leadership Conference. In December 2019, Dr. Green and I spoke by phone, and he extended an invitation to hear him speak in Atlanta during the January 2020 Dr. Martin Luther King holiday (Figure I.1). During our visit, I was able to sit down and speak at length about his book *At the Crossroads of Fear and Freedom: The Fight for Social and Educational Justice* and his research experiences in Prince Edward County, Virginia. Dr. Green and his researchers from Michigan State University received a grant funded by the US Office of Education to study the impact that the Prince Edward County school closing had on Black youth. Dr. Green and associates provided findings of low IQ scores for Black children affected by the county's school lockout.

Figure I.1

Former Deans Dr. Terence Hicks and Dr. Robert Green. *Atlanta, Georgia*

Source: The King Center for Nonviolent Social Change. Image provided by Caselove Productions.

The collection of studies in this book contributes greatly to the research literature surrounding the Prince Edward County School closing. It is my hope that this edited volume can contribute to the knowledge base in the humanities, history, psychology, and education and can be adopted by many high schools and universities and used as supplemental reading material for courses such as US History; Equity, Inclusion, and Social Justice; African American History; and Black Studies and Explorations.

In 2005, Virginia sponsored a restorative justice policy known as the *Brown v. Board of Education* Scholarship Program and Fund (the *Brown* Scholarship Fund). The *Brown* Scholarship Fund aimed to restore education to those denied public-school education as part of Virginia's government resistance strategies to *Brown* (1954). From 1959 to 1964, Prince Edward County effectively closed their schools to avoid desegregation, resulting in the denial of education to thousands of Black students. In Chapter 1, Linda J. Mann explores the justice potential of the *Brown* Scholarship Fund through 14 ethnographic case studies. Findings demonstrated that the voices of those wronged were muffled through policy design. As a result, the *Brown* Scholarship Fund did not respond to the needs of those impacted by the school closings. Policymaking often occurred in segregated spaces and further diminished the justice potential of the scholarship fund. Recommendations on restorative justice policymaking are provided.

Chapter 2 by Emily Martin Cochran argues that Prince Edward County's role in *Brown v. Board of Education* is often overlooked in scholarship and public memory, as Virginia was often deemed "moderate" on civil rights. A close examination of the papers of Prince Edward's and Virginia's White segregationists shows that these men took extreme measures to resist court-ordered integration and also created a framework for other segregationists to use across the country. In examining more recent efforts to collect oral histories from Black Prince Edward County students and leaders, Cochran argues that these sources show how Prince Edward's local civil rights movement influenced other communities across the South.

In Chapter 3, Dwana Waugh uses oral histories, reflections, and newspaper accounts to trace the intersections of public remembering of massive resistance in Prince Edward County. She argues that saving Robert Russa Moton symbolized an opportunity for the county's Blacks and Whites to reconcile the acrimony of the past and that the preservation of R. R. Moton High School would transform the county from a narrative of racial intransigence to a narrative of racial healing. Moton would stand as a treasured, and important, national landmark.

Chapter 4, by Caitlin B. Maloney, outlines pedagogical methods for teaching about the Civil Rights Movement and Prince Edward County, Virginia, in K-12 spaces. Maloney argues that primary-source-based instruction fosters greater levels of student engagement and success. She then provides an overview of a primary-source-based curriculum found in "A Microhistory of Prince Edward County, Virginia, 1951–1964: Civil Rights Curriculum for Virginia's Secondary Educators" to provide educators with examples of how to teach about Prince Edward County in their own classrooms.

In Chapter 5, Jeffrey Carlton Scales uses a case study to explore concerns about lower academic and social achievement of current Black students in Prince Edward County Public Schools. This qualitative study was conducted to gather data from 10 participants who had firsthand knowledge of the extended closure of public schools. Scales utilized face-to-face interviews, focus groups, and extensive historical documentation to explore the residual effects from the 5-year public school closure and its impact on the accomplishments of Black children in Prince Edward County today.

In Chapter 6, Rory Dunn outlines how oral history can be used as a tool for accessing silenced narratives and addressing difficult knowledge. Through this process, Dunn engages with theories of narrative silences and difficult knowledge/difficult history by using his oral history work with the Prince Edward County school closures. The chapter ends with suggestions for teachers working where historical trauma has fractured communities.

Chapter 7, written by Alicia Pennington, examines the growing scholarship in the emergent field of geographies of education and its relationship to "place." Pennington notes that the field has expanded since its beginning in the 1970s as a key subdiscipline of human geography in education analysis. To situate the Prince Edward County school closings in Farmville, Virginia, from 1959 to 1964 on the analytic perimeters of the field of geographies of education, "place" becomes a critical area of study. Through the examination of interdisciplinary literature, Pennington not only develops a synthesis of the historical significance of the acquisition of education in the lives of African Americans in Virginia broadly but also presents the possibilities of delivering additional understandings of "place" as an investigative area.

References

Hicks, T. (2021). *An educational journey to deanship: A memoir.* Hamilton Books.

Hicks, T., & Pitre, A. (2010). *The educational lockout of African Americans in Prince Edward County, Virginia (1959–1964): Personal accounts and reflections.* University Press of America.

Wright, C. (Photograph). (2020). *Former Deans Dr. Terence Hicks and Dr. Robert Green* (Photograph). Atlanta, Georgia. Photo credit: The King Center for Nonviolent Social Change image provided by Caselove Productions.

Additional Reading

April 23, 1951: 16-Year-Old Barbara Johns leads a student strike. https.www.zinnedproject.org/news/tdih/Barbara-johns-leads0student-protest/

CHAPTER 1

THE POTENTIAL OF GOVERNMENT-SPONSORED RESTORATIVE JUSTICE: A US CASE STUDY OF THE *BROWN* SCHOLARSHIP FUND

Linda J. Mann
Columbia University, USA

Introduction

The Brown *Scholarship Fund: Historical Injustice to Contemporary Redress*

The intent of *Brown* (1954) was to set schools on a path to desegregation resulting in greater educational opportunities for Black students. However, *Brown*'s (1954) vague Supreme Court ruling allowed for state and local interpretations that supported resistance and the denial of desegregation (Patterson, 2001). Southern states that once constituted the Confederacy developed strong resistance policies to prevent and contain integration (Sweeney, 2008). Virginia led the way (Cochran, 2006). Among many resistance policies, Virginia repealed its compulsory education mandate, thus allowing students to evade an integrated school setting (Bonastia, 2012).

Five Virginia localities—Warren and Prince Edward counties and the cities of Norfolk, Arlington, and Charlottesville—applied this policy to their oversight of public education (Cochran, 2006). Local officials argued that if students were not required to attend public schools, then communities were not required to provide public schooling.

Out of the five localities, Prince Edward County had a unique history. It was the site of *Davis v. County School Board of Prince Edward* (1952), one of the five legal cases that comprised *Brown*. Yet, despite the county's role in *Brown*, the board of supervisors adopted an intransigent position against desegregation and successfully closed their schools from 1959 to 1964 (Bonastia, 2012). To further their segregated agenda, the Prince Edward County board of supervisors utilized other resistance policies to fund a White-only private school and, accordingly, secured education for the majority-White student population (Fuquay, 2002). Consequently, approximately 2,400 Black students and some poor White students did not receive formal schooling unless they sought education outside of the county (Peeples, 2004). Prince Edward County public schools were reopened with *Griffin v. County School Board of Prince Edward County* (1964), which declared the school closures unconstitutional.

Research on the Prince Edward County school closures demonstrated that the educational impact for the Black students was considerable. The Department of Health, Education, and Welfare sponsored a research team in 1963 from Michigan State University to explore the educational impact. Researchers performed interviews, parent surveys, and educational assessments. This research demonstrated that students were academically delayed; many struggled with literacy (Green et al., 1964). Peeples's (1963) analysis of local government policies reported similar findings, indicating that as many as three-fourths of affected students did not participate in formal education during the school closures. Many students were unsuccessful in their return to school or in attaining a high school degree (Green et al., 1967).

The loss of an education impacted the students' economic and employment potential. Heaton (2008) combined administrative data on the Prince Edward County displaced students to assess the long-term outcomes of a denied education. The results of Heaton's study suggested that older students lost 4 years of educational attainment compared to Black students from neighboring school systems with similar demographics. Heaton also reported that the loss of an education placed individuals below the poverty line throughout adulthood. Hale-Smith (1993) surveyed over 100 displaced Prince Edward County students and reported similar findings: as adults, the students had below-average income levels and worked in low-skilled jobs.

Turner (2004) explored the socioemotional impact of the school closings. She reported that students experienced social exclusion, separation from families, and the loss of other childhood norms. Long-term, the lack of an education resulted in feelings of humiliation and a deep mourning.

In the 1990s, after years of silence within the Prince Edward community, government officials announced the potential razing of the original, Black-only school, the Robert Russa (R.R.) Moton High School. The potential loss of this community landmark, which also served as the site of the *Davis v. County* (1952) case, stirred the emotions of Black community members. One of its longstanding Black-led, grassroots groups, the Martha E. Forrester Council, rallied the community to preserve the school. Their efforts successfully established the school as a national historic site and the formation of the R.R. Moton Civil Rights in Education Museum. The preservation of the historic school coincided with the 50th anniversary of *Brown* and spurred Virginia policymakers to visit the R.R. Moton Museum and, accordingly, address their role in the school closures (Bonastia, 2012). In 2003, the General Assembly conveyed regret for the historic school closings (House Joint Resolution no. 613, 2003).

Although the statement of regret was welcomed by the Prince Edward County community, Black-led organizations continued to push the General Assembly to create a scholarship program as a form of repair (Woodley, 2019). Again, community members mobilized and formed an effort known as the Get on the Bus Campaign. This campaign received media attention when five school buses of 50- to 70-year-old displaced students and community members traveled to the General Assembly to approve reparations (Titus, 2011). The Virginia legislature responded with the restorative justice policy known as The *Brown v. Board of Education* Scholarship Program and Fund (HB 846, 2004), hereafter referred to as the *Brown* Scholarship Fund. The *Brown* Scholarship Fund offered scholarships to Virginians denied an education between 1954 and 1964. Awards were provided to only those directly denied an education. Funds were to be used for enrollment at an accredited school as outlined by the Virginia Constitution, Article VIII, and required in-state residency ("Eligibility for in-state tuition charges," 2011–2013). $2,050,000 was apportioned for the *Brown* Scholarship Fund.

The *Brown* Scholarship Fund was analyzed theoretically by Walker (2006) and Williams (2005). Williams (2005) determined that the program fell short of providing adequate reparations for the damages incurred. Walker (2006) explored several local restorative justice policies and listed the *Brown* Scholarship Fund as an example. However, these analyses were void of the voices of those wronged.

Framing

To assure that the rights and privileges of Black Americans are at the forefront, practitioners and scholars often apply critical race theory (CRT) as a policy framework (Delgado & Stefancic, 2012). CRT uses counter narratives by those who have experienced injustices to protect marginalized communities and push back against the prevalence of racism (Matsuda, 1987;

Stovall, 2006). The application of CRT is particularly warranted when determining the justice potential of policymaking aimed to attend to historical racial injustices (Yamamoto, 1997, 1998). Yamamoto (1997) applied CRT to the practice of restorative justice and deemed it *critical race praxis*. He presented that restorative justice framed within CRT might better support racial reconciliation and redress within communities directly wronged (1998). Further, he suggested that restorative justice might redirect large-scale monetary compensations and attend to societal rifts caused by racism.

However, the analysis of restorative justice initiatives has proven to be challenging due to the lack of theoretical and design clarity. Restorative justice policies often vary in both depth and breadth depending on the needs of the community and those initiating the redress (Zehr, 2002). Walgrave (2011) suggested that in order to assess the varying types of initiatives, the analyses of restorative justice should be based on victim satisfaction and program outcomes. Walgrave asserted that restorative justice evaluations should explore the initial feelings of those involved in the development of restorative justice. Analyses should also assess programs during their implementation as well as the long-term experiences of the victims. Walgrave stressed that because restorative justice emphasizes the needs of victims, analyzing programs based on recipients' perceptions and experiences keeps the marginalized population at the forefront. In this way, researchers can gain a better understanding of a restorative justice program's success, shortcomings, or partial repair.

Utilizing the frameworks of CRT and Walgrave's analysis protocol, this study explored the perceptions and lived experiences of 14 displaced students and later scholarship recipients. Each displaced student served as a case study. This research was further analyzed alongside archival data pertaining to the school closings. In addition, legislative action performed by the *Brown* Scholarship Fund Committee was assessed. Finally, instrumental case analysis was used to explore potential recurring themes among all cases. The research questions reflected Walgrave's (2011) analysis framework and are as follows:

Q1. What were the Prince Edward County Black scholarship recipients' initial perceptions of the *Brown* Scholarship Fund?
Q2. What, if any, impact did the *Brown* Scholarship Fund have on the lives of the recipients?
Q3. What, if any, suggestions might the displaced students offer to secure restorative justice through the scholarship program?

Methods and Data Collection

Prince Edward County was selected as the site of study due to its lengthy and persistent quest to maintain segregated education (Hicks & Pitre, 2010).

This study included extensive archival research, a policy analysis of the *Brown* Scholarship Fund, and 14 ethnographic case studies based on the perspectives and lived experiences of individuals denied an education during the 1959–1964 closure of Prince Edward County Schools.

Archival-type research was performed from July 2012 to December 2013 and resulted in the analysis of approximately 380 documents relevant to the case. Documents assessed included those of the National Association for the Advancement of Colored People held at the Library of Congress. These papers provided historical context for the legal battle to reopen Prince Edward County Schools. They also provided evidence of the Black community's efforts to secure equal access to public education in the 1950s resulting in Prince Edward County's role as one of the five legal cases that comprised *Brown v. Board* (1954). The aforementioned Martha E. Forrester Council was noted multiple times throughout archival documents. This was the same grassroots organization that was pivotal in securing R.R. Moton High School in the 1990s as a historic preservation site and later a museum dedicated to the fight for civil rights in education.

To understand the legislative efforts for the *Brown* Scholarship Fund, committee meetings were attended at the Virginia State Capitol in Richmond from June 2013 to December 2014. Field notes were recorded. Legislative documents were also acquired including financial reports and other pertinent data.

As mentioned, the preservation of R.R. Moton High School resulted in the creation of a civil rights in education museum, the R.R. Moton Museum. This site offered numerous community gatherings and served as an entrance to the Black community. Table 1.1 provides an overview of the activities attended to develop trust with the Prince Edward County community.

After this author logged time and demonstrated trustworthiness (Glesne, 2011), a member of Prince Edward County offered a list of scholarship recipients who possibly would be willing to discuss their experience.

Because participants were older adults, potential participants were contacted via the US Postal Service (Patterson & Dupree, 1994). Over one hundred (107) letters were mailed with self-addressed stamped envelopes, and 24 individuals responded within a four-week timeframe: 5 males and 19 females. All five males were selected to provide as great a gender perspective as possible. The youngest and oldest female respondents were chosen with the remaining participants randomly selected. Table 1.2 provides participant demographics and indicates whether each participant attained a degree by means of the *Brown* Scholarship Fund.

All participants reviewed an Institutional Review Board-approved consent form and agreed to provide various documents pertaining to their award of the *Brown* Scholarship Fund. Additionally, each participant took part in an in-depth ethnographic interview to record and preserve their lived experiences (Englander, 2012). An interview guide was designed

Table 1.1

Gaining Access

Event	Location	Date(s)
Tredegar Civil War Presentation	The American Civil War Center at Historic Tredegar 500 Tredegar St, Richmond, VA 23219	February 21, 2013
Brown Scholarship Fund Committee Meetings	Virginia General Assembly 1000 Bank St, Richmond, VA 23218	June 19, 2013 July 15, 2013 December 13, 2013 February 11, 2014 August 15, 2014 December 10, 2014
Annual Moton Community Awards Banquet	Hampden-Sydney College 1 College Rd, Farmville, VA 23901	October 17, 2013 October 2, 2014
R.R. Moton Alumni Banquet	Twin Lakes State Park 788 Twin Lakes Road Green Bay, VA 23942	April 26, 2013
Brown Bag Lunch Meetings	Robert Russa Moton Museum 900 Griffin Blvd, Farmville, VA 23901	May 6, 2013 August 29, 2013 September 9, 2013 September 23, 2013 October 28, 2013 February 10, 2014 March 31, 2014 June 23, 2014 August 18, 2014 October 20, 2014

Note: These data do not include interview dates, which are provided in Table 1.2.

that required participants to describe and make sense of their experiences (Maxwell, 2009). An initial pilot interview was performed with a member from the museum to ensure that the research questions were addressed (Sampson, 2004). Great care was taken to secure a comfortable interviewing setting, including the local library and other community locations. Site locations and interview descriptions are provided in Table 1.3.

Each participant was analyzed as a separate case followed by a cross-case analysis to explore the "interactivity" of the data (Merriam, 2009;

Table 1.2
Characteristics of Participants

Pseudonym	Gender	Age	Degree via *Brown Scholarship Fund*	Post High School Degree	Career
Suzanne	F	65	Yes	Bachelor of science (BS), business administration, St. Paul's College; master's in executive leadership, Liberty University	Writer, current; public school employee, retired
Cheryl	F	63	Yes	BS, business administration, St. Paul's College	Writer, current; firefighter, retired
John	M	62	Yes	BS, business administration, St. Paul's College	Bus driver, current; air force, retired
Rose	F	65	Yes	BS, business administration, St. Paul's College	Public school employee, current; factory worker, retired
Judy	F	68	Yes	BS, business administration, St. Paul's College	Writing memoirs, current; human resource specialist, retired
Jean	F	58	Yes	Master's in executive leadership, human services, counseling minor, Liberty University; BS, business administration, St. Paul's College; general education development	Virginia department of social services, local division, 30 years, current
Wilma	F	64	No	BSN, Lynchburg College; licensed practical nurse; general education development	RN, current
Joe	M	58	Yes	BS, business administration, St. Paul's College	Small business owner; on disability

(Continued)

Table 1.2 (Continued)

Pseudonym	Gender	Age	Degree via *Broum* Scholarship Fund	Post High School Degree	Career
Ellie	F	65	No	BS, Johnson C. Smith College	Author, current; government employee, retired
Miles	M	62	Yes	Master's student, counseling, Virginia State University; BS, business administration, St. Paul's College	Mental health counselor, current
Debbie	F	63	No	Licensed practical nurse, Southside Community College	Health care provider retirement facility, current
Sally	F	67	Yes	BS, business administration, St. Paul's College	Supervisor at local prison, food services, current
Carol	F	62	Yes	BS, business administration, St. Paul's College; previous course work, Southside Community College, Liberty University	Social worker, current
Mike	M	65	Yes	BS, business administration, St. Paul's College; associate's degree, John Tyler community college	Local business owner, current.

Table 1.3

Interview Descriptions

Pseudonym	Date and Time	Location	Length
Suzanne	December 18, 2015, 12:00 PM	Midlothian Restaurant	1:08:47
Cheryl	December 3, 2015, 3:00 PM	Farmville-Prince Edward Community Library	1:12:06
John	November 20, 2015, 11:00 PM	Farmville-Prince Edward Community Library	43:32
Rose	November 20, 2015, 4:00 PM	Farmville-Prince Edward Community Library	52:26
Judy	November 24, 2015, 1:30 PM	Farmville-Prince Edward Community Library	50:35
Jean	December 11, 2015, 11:00 PM	Farmville-Prince Edward Community Library	51:36
Wilma	December 11, 2015, 3:30 PM	Home, Farmville	41:57
Joe	December 11, 2015, 6:00 PM	Phone	47:41
Ellie	November 20, 2015, 1:30 PM	Farmville restaurant	55:00
Miles	November 24, 2015, 10:00 AM	Farmville-Prince Edward Community Library	58:29
Debbie	December 15, 2015, 12:30 PM	Farmville-Prince Edward Community Library	46:59
Rose	December 15, 2015, 10:00 AM	Farmville-Prince Edward Community Library	52:26
Carol	December 15, 2015, 3:00 PM	Farmville-Prince Edward Community Library	43:31
Mike	December 18, 2015, 5:00 PM	Midlothian Restaurant	1:04:03

Note: The average interview lasted 61.88 minutes.

Stake, 2005). Interviews were transcribed verbatim. This process served as part of the analysis process (Roulston, 2010). Key phrases or words were coded and placed into categories such as the importance of valuing an education or the generational impact of the school closings.

The development of theoretical categories was done alongside the analysis of the archival data, the *Brown* Scholarship Fund committee documents, analytical memos, and field notes (Maxwell, 2005). A total of 52 audio field notes and 33 composition-sized pages of handwritten notes were taken during the study. Field notes and analytical memos were used to verify and interpret interview data. Several audiotaped analytical memos challenged assumptions (Mason, 2002).

The final step of analysis explored the relationships that existed between and within the cases (Yin, 2009) and situated the data within the framework of restorative justice and the analysis of outcomes, as suggested by Walgrave (2011). One example was the comparison of an analytical memo discussing the *Brown* Scholarship Fund's focus on economic transformation through the award of a scholarship (Field note, April 23, 2014). This memo was analyzed alongside interview data and legislative documents, which demonstrated significant concerns that the scholarship did not attend to the community rifts that were created because of the historic school closings. This category was later termed *restoration unfulfilled* and is discussed as part of the next section in *Findings*.

Findings

This study, framed within CRT, appropriately placed the voices of those wronged at the forefront of the analysis. A cross-case analysis explored the interactivity within all case studies to further understand the restorative justice potential of the *Brown* Scholarship Fund. The following presents the findings and first reports on the Prince Edward County Black scholarship recipients' perceptions and the impact of the *Brown* Scholarship Fund. Findings specific to the individual scholarship experiences demonstrated the following: (a) age-mitigated material benefits, (b) literacy exclusion, (c) personal growth, and (d) racial divide. The analysis of the *Brown* Scholarship Fund's restorative justice potential demonstrated a lack of attention to (a) emotional harms, (b) excluded displaced populations, (c) making history visible, and (d) the next generation.

Age-Mitigated Impact

All 14 cases demonstrated that age mitigated the impact of the *Brown* Scholarship Fund, and therefore there was a lack of economic or material gain. Although 11 of the 14 interviewees completed advanced degrees because of the scholarship program, participants countered that as older adults they were unable to reap any financial or vocational advancement. According to Mike, one of the founders involved in the initial drafting of the *Brown* Scholarship Fund, the policy goal was "to improve everyone's economic condition." However, only three participants discussed any occupational or financial change. Suzanne, who worked for the public school system, received a small stipend but retired 2 years later. Jean and Miles reported that they became licensed professional counselors but were unwilling to change their locations of employment due to age and family commitments. The remaining participants reported they were preparing for retirement. Wilma reported, "You know you're not going to change and go back to school and get another career at 50 or 60 years old."

Literacy Exclusion

Further, all 14 members reported that the *Brown* Scholarship Fund had limited reach and was unobtainable for most displaced students. Participants unanimously agreed that they were fortunate to have completed a high school degree despite the school closings and that their own literacy was essential to obtaining a scholarship. Jean emphasized her efforts to assure literacy: "I knew I couldn't spell and so I knew I had to get that poor little dictionary out and spell things." Rose spoke about her literacy struggle: "If the public knew, you know, my poor reading skills and my poor spelling skills they would probably be surprised. But I just pushed my way through."

Participants highlighted that policymakers should have known that literacy remained a challenge for displaced students, as most schoolchildren were unable to secure formal educational opportunities during the school closures (Peeples, 2004). Past investigations reported high levels of illiteracy among Prince Edward County displaced students (Green et al., 1967; Green & Hoffmann, 1965; Hicks & Pitre, 2010). All 14 participants stated that policymakers made assumptions that displaced students were literate. Participants quantified that individuals needed advanced reading skills just to complete the application. Wilma reported, "A lot of the people from the school closings can't read or write, so who's going to fill those [scholarship applications] out?"

Literacy also came in the form of understanding the *Brown* Scholarship Fund application system. Eight of the participants reported that recipients had to learn how to successfully navigate the application process. Individuals reported the need to call the senior research associate for Virginia's Division of Legislative Services (2005) to inquire about the application. Three participants discussed the difficulties they had in acquiring their 1950–1960 high school transcripts to prove they were displaced students.

Personal Growth

Despite the evidence that the scholarship program failed to provide material gain, recipients reported personal growth and satisfaction. Sally recollected the pride she felt from the aforementioned Get on the Bus Campaign, the campaign forwarded by Black community members to advocate for the scholarship by testifying to the state legislature during legislative hearings. "They got us off the bus and we went on in and sat down ... and we got to listen to everything that was going on in the Assembly." Several students discussed going back to school. Suzanne said, "It was really nice 'cause that [going back to school] was something I always wanted to do." Rose stated similarly, "I always wanted to go [to college]."

Recipients also conveyed the pride they felt by completing their degrees. Mike stated, "Graduating had special significance. Now we were pushing to succeed despite all the odds that we had put against us. And that probably meant more than anything." Suzanne conveyed, "The feeling that you get walking and standing with thousands of people ... that really made me feel like I had achieved." Carol declared, "Pride! That's all I can tell you. ... I just didn't think that I was able to achieve that. And it took me a long time to get there."

Seven individuals stated that they gained a sense of empowerment by improving skills. Sally discussed her reading progress: "I mean I learned my vocabulary. You know my reading skills, everything, because I really had to buckle down and get it." Joe discussed the skills he gained with his business degree: "I was really glad though because it gave you more of an outlook on business and financial reports."

Five of the participants discussed that the scholarship experience made them visible. Ellie stated that when she was in college in the 1970s, she was embarrassed by the school closings, but now as a scholarship recipient, she was no longer silent. Miles stated that it restored his self-esteem. Cheryl recalled, "We cried so much together, just things that would come out that probably hadn't come out and people needed to get out." Rose summarized, "It made me feel like somebody else knew how we felt."

Racial Divide

There was a unanimous sentiment, however, that any success obtained because of the *Brown* Scholarship Fund was made possible by the Black community's cultural capital. Participants stated that the Black community was greatly responsible for the creation of the policy and therefore lessened the sincerity of the program's justice potential. Members posed that the Prince Edward County community's grassroots efforts such as the Get on the Bus Campaign were impactful to the passing of the bill.

Mike reported that several key Black community leaders, including himself, worked with the Black Caucus to draft the *Brown* Scholarship Fund and assure its passage. Mike said, "Before people got involved with the Get on the Bus Campaign, before that even happened, there was a lot going on to determine the value of it and draft the legislation for it within the Black community." Mike further discussed how the scholarship program began:

> I was working a lot through the Martha E. Forrester Council of Women, a Black community organization. The Council was in place when the first Black-only high school was built. ... There were about 10 or 12 meetings, and it took us over a year to draft the scholarship.

Suzanne confirmed Mike's report and stated that prior to the Get on the Bus Campaign there was a concerted effort by the Black community. "The main people who had started it, we would have meetings and we decided to gather people in the community and the surrounding community." Ellie further elaborated that influencing the General Assembly was the agenda of the Get on the Bus Campaign. "That's what the whole conversation was about. Everyone was driven by the fact that we needed, they [the General Assembly] needed to do more than say sorry."

Ellie and Mike expressed frustration that these efforts were without support from the White community despite attempts to build a coalition. They discussed at length that information was sent to both Black and White community churches requesting support. Ellie reported, "No White churches responded, and it's because of—I can't say exactly, I feel like—it's because of what's happened and people still trying to cover things up." They stated that this act and similar responses to the scholarship program demonstrated continued racism.

The White churches were not the only institutions that dismissed the *Brown* Scholarship Fund. Further evidence demonstrated that there was little to no buy-in from local White colleges and institutions. Participants presented that two state-approved, higher-education institutions located within a 10-mile radius of the museum did nothing to support the scholarship program. Jean reported, "Other universities nearby did not appear to be very receptive." Joe shared, "And nobody, none of the other colleges in the area said anything." Suzanne stated, "Other universities didn't try to make accommodations for us to have classrooms or anything like that."

Participants presented that the only school that put forth great effort to respond to the scholarship program was St. Paul's College, a Historic Black College and University located in Lawrenceville, Virginia, 60 miles from Prince Edward County. Moreover, it was St. Paul's who considered the needs of the older displaced students by establishing a satellite program that offered two bachelor's degree options at the R.R. Moton Museum. According to the participants, the lack of buy-in by the White institutions lessened their perceptions of restorative justice.

Out of the 14 participants, 11 members successfully completed an advanced degree through the St. Paul's program and reported that the satellite program was key to their success. Wilma reported, "Even bringing the school to the people, even then it was difficult." Joe discussed the difficulties in closing his store early even to attend local classes. Suzanne stated, "The only reason I was able to go was because they came to Prince Edward County and taught us in the walls of the Moton Museum." The three remaining participants who used their scholarship award to go to institutions other than St. Paul's reported that their age and traveling to a distant community resulted in their inability to complete their degrees.

To verify the success and impact of the St. Paul's program, the *Brown* Scholarship Fund Committee reported that close to 50% of the total funds dispersed as of December 2013 went to the satellite program offered by St. Paul's (*Brown v. Board of Education* Scholarship Program and Fund Committee, 2013a, 2013b). The two local predominantly White neighboring universities were not mentioned on their funding report. Unfortunately for future scholarship recipients, St. Paul ceased operations in 2013 due to a loss of accreditation (Hawkins, 2013). Committee members cited its closure as the reason for a significant decrease in scholarship applications (December 2014).

Socioemotional Harm

When participants discussed the term *restorative justice*, they communicated that restoring justice meant much more than a monetary contribution toward their lost education. Judy directly addressed the term *education restoration*, stating, "Education restoration doesn't mean a whole lot. I don't think we are restoring anything." Cheryl added that the emphasis of the *Brown* Scholarship Fund was on education, but there was more to restore. She continued,

> This program does not recognize the effect not going to school had on the Prince Edward County students who were deprived an education and the trauma it caused. Healing is not all about going back to school and an education. This community is still so broken.

Mike shared similar sentiments, stating, "You can't replace what's done and you can never recapture the damage or undo the damage that's done." Suzanne spoke directly to her regret that she could not attend college in her youth. She reflected, "That's the hurting part, I mean, you know, that whether you think about it or not, you will never know what you would have done, or you could have been 'cause that was taken away from you." Finally, Wilma challenged the intentions of the policy: "Whom are you restoring for? And who is deciding what is being restored? It shouldn't be restoration. That shouldn't be the word they are using."

Participants unanimously discussed that the *Brown* Scholarship Fund excluded out-of-state displaced students. Evidence demonstrated that many students were forced to move out of Virginia during the historic school closures to seek an education elsewhere (Brinson, 2004; Peeples, 2004). Rose expressed that three of her sisters remained out-of-state despite the reopening of schools in 1964. She stated they wanted to participate in the scholarship program, but their out-of-state residency denied them an education yet again. She expanded her statement that her sisters were not alone and stated, "A lot of people who left when the schools closed, never came back." Participants suggested that at the very least, out-of-state students should be able to take online Virginia-approved programs.

Make History Known

Although several participants reported that they were no longer silent about their personal loss of an education, they stated there was a need for the Prince Edward County history to be known by the greater public. Further, even though the history was becoming part of Virginia public school curriculum, they questioned the reliability of the lessons. They challenged that no one from the Virginia Department of Education sought their firsthand knowledge of this historic event.

The Next Generation

Participants reported that their intentions for the *Brown* Scholarship Fund was always to create a scholarship program for the next generation. Individuals reported that both the Black Caucus and the Get on the Bus Campaign advocated for this policy. They cited the generational impact and their age as the reasons why they wanted the scholarship to go to the next generation. John said, "There could have been a smarter use cause it's just a piece of paper at my age." Mike expressed frustration that the Virginia legislators did not consider their policy recommendations. He posed that if congresspeople had taken the advisement of the displaced students and the Black Caucus, they would have understood that disbursing scholarships to direct descendants would potentially transform the long-term impact of Virginia's racist transgressions.

Summary

Findings from this study demonstrated that the *Brown* Scholarship Fund resulted in unfulfilled restorative justice. Participants were too old for the program to offer material gain. Interviewees also cited that literacy was essential to obtaining a scholarship, and yet most displaced students struggled with literacy. Individuals who received scholarships and completed a degree reported personal fulfillment. However, scholarship recipients presented that the attainment of their degree was realized solely because of St. Paul's satellite program. The justice potential of the scholarship program was also lessened because its creation and limited success were largely dependent on the segregated efforts of the Black community.

Participants reported that to provide meaningful restorative justice, policies must attend to both emotional and material losses. Policies must be inclusive and attend to as many members as possible that were affected by past wrongdoings. Making history visible is important, but the retelling of this history must place the voices of those wronged at the forefront. Finally, the generational impact must be paramount in restorative justice policymaking. In the case of the *Brown* Scholarship Fund, this would have resulted in designing the scholarship program to go to the next generation.

Perplexing to these findings was the fact that avenues existed to implement the participants' policy suggestions. The *Brown* Scholarship Fund Committee was required to engage with "the Board of Education, Virginia Community College System, State Council of Higher Education, public and private institutions of higher education" (Title 30. VA General Assembly, 2010, para. 5) to make sure the program was administered according to the bylaws. Further, the State Council of Higher Education approved a Statewide Strategic Plan for Higher Education that offered guidance for institutes to implement initiatives committed to (a) degree completion and lifelong learning, (b) scholarship and diversity, and (c) expansion of participation and engagement in public service and institutional service to the community (State Council of Higher Education for Virginia, 2014). Therefore, under this framework, systems already existed for the *Brown* Scholarship Fund to promote the policies suggested by the displaced students. This finding has implications for the way the scholarship was designed and is suggestive that the design of the restorative justice policy as envisioned by the Black community was realizable but dismissed.

Discussion

As the United States enters an era of attending to historical racist transgressions, this study has great value. Efforts to address historical wrongdoings are evident in the creation of new museums such as the Legacy Museum (EJI, 2019) and the Universities Studying Slavery consortium, where 60-plus universities and colleges are examining their slave past and developing policies of atonement (Rector and Visitors of the University of Virginia, 2020). As we embark on these initiatives, we must consider how policymakers develop restorative justice acts and question whether they are designed to attend to the voices of those wronged. Although not generalizable, this study presents that when restorative justice policies are developed solely within existing US institutional structures, they remain prey to White hegemony resulting in unfulfilled repair. The following are brief policy suggestions that may help to assure the development of meaningful repair.

Policy Recommendations

If policymakers are truly invested in restorative justice, those wronged should play a vital role in the creation and implementation of restorative justice policies. Further, as demonstrated, members of the wronged community can offer clear and realizable policy solutions. During the design, execution, and evaluation of restorative justice policymaking, the voices of the disenfranchised must be given equal standing.

As suggested, in order for restorative justice policies to develop a sense of justice, initiatives might also attend to the less-tangible losses. Participants elaborated that the lifelong struggle of being illiterate not only equated to financial and vocational loss but also resulted in emotional anguish. As suggested by the participants of this study, education was only one piece of what needed to be restored.

Bittker (1973) posed that reparations should focus on wrongdoings committed within the last century. However, the findings from this study suggested that if restorative justice programs are to go to those directly wronged, they must be developed in a timelier manner. Participants from this study reported that too much time had passed between the creation of the restorative justice policy and the historic school closures to maximize the effectiveness of the program and, accordingly, rebuild their lives (Wenzel et al., 2008). As stated by Suzanne, "Sometimes late is never." If restorative justice policies are not implemented in a timely manner, then the generational impact must be the focus. Policymakers' denial to distribute funds to the next generation or their undervaluing and dismissal of the generational impact only demonstrates yet another rejection of attending to the needs of those wronged and exasperates racial tensions and societal rifts.

Conclusion

This study suggests that if the voices of those wronged are not at the forefront of restorative justice policymaking, then efforts may fall short and, in some cases, perpetuate existing racial division and segregation. However, as stated by Zehr (2002), restorative justice policymaking is varied and on a continuum. Therefore, the efforts by Virginia should not be dismissed. This was a historic restorative justice act that offered reparations in the form of a scholarship program. Since this study, the Commonwealth ruled to allow descendants of those directly impacted by the school closings to apply to the *Brown* Scholarship Fund. This decision warrants future research to determine the impact on the next generation. Through the analysis of such efforts, the US can learn what steps are necessary to provide meaningful repair.

References

Bittker, B. I. (1973). *The case for Black reparations*. Random House.

Bonastia, C. (2012). *Southern stalemate: Five years without public education in Prince Edward County, Virginia* [Kindle DX version]. University of Chicago Press.

Brinson, B. (2004). The AFSC and school desegregation: Prince Edward County, Virginia, 1959–1964. *Friends Journal*. http://mlkcommission.dls.virginia.gov/va_school_closings/pdfs/AFSC_and_school_desegregation.pdf

Brown v. Board of Education of Topeka, 347 US 483 (1954).

Brown v. Board of Education Scholarship Program and Fund Committee. (2013a, July 9). *Proceedings on fiscal status report*. Fifth Floor West Conference Room. General Assembly Building, Richmond, Virginia.

Brown v. Board of Education Scholarship Program and Fund Committee. (2013b, December 10). *Fiscal status report*. Fifth Floor West Conference Room. General Assembly Building, Richmond, Virginia.

Cochran, G. M. (2006). Virginia facing reality: The 1959 Perrow Commission. *Augusta Historical Bulletin, 42*, 1–13. http://www.newsleader.com/assets/pdf/AA169360123.PDF

Davis v. County School Bd. of Prince Edward County, D.C., 149 F. Supp. 431. (1952).

Delgado, R., & Stefancic, J. (2012). *Critical race theory: An introduction*. New York University Press.

Eligibility for in-state tuition charges. (2011–2013). https://vacode.org/23-7.4

EJI. (2019). Legacy museum: From enslavement to mass incarceration. https://eji.org/legacy-museum

Englander, M. (2012). The interview: Data collection in descriptive phenomenological human scientific research. *Journal of Phenomenological Psychology, 43*(1), 13–35. https://doi.org/10.1163/156916212x632943

Field note. (2014, April 23). Audiotaped note on repair and economics. Ethnographic interviews, Farmville Community Library, Farmville, VA.

Fuquay, M. W. (2002). Civil rights and the private school movement in Mississippi, 1964–1971. *History of Education Quarterly, 42*(2), 159–180. https://doi.org/10.1111/j.1748-5959.2002.tb00105.x

Glesne, C. (2011). *Becoming qualitative researchers: An introduction* (4th ed.). Longman.

Green, R. L., & Hoffmann, L. J. (1965). A case study of the effects of educational deprivation on southern rural Negro children. *The Journal of Negro Education, 34*(3), 327–341.

Green, R. L., Hoffmann, L. J., & Morgan, R. F. (1967). Some effects of deprivation on intelligence, achievement, and cognitive growth. *The Journal of Negro Education, 36*(1), 5–14. https://doi.org/10.2307/2294559

Green, R. L., Hoffmann, L. J., Morse, R. J., Hayes, M. E., & Morgan, R. F. (1964). *The educational status of children in a district without public schools*. Cooperative Research Project No. 2321. Department of Health, Education and Welfare, US Office of Education.

Griffin v. County School Board of Prince Edward County—377 US 218. (1964). I, p. 377 US 228 Judicial Code of 1911 as amended, 28 US C. (1934 ed.) (§ 380). http://supreme.justia.com/cases/federal/us/377/218/case.html. Accessed on February 2, 2013.

Hale-Smith, M. E. (1993). The effect of early educational disruption on the belief systems and educational practices of adults: Another look at the prince. Edward county school closings. *The Journal of Negro Education, 62*(2), 171–189. http://doi.org/10.2307/2295192

Hawkins, D. B. (2013, June 30). After 125 years of service, St. Paul's College shutting down. *Diverse: Issues in Higher Education.* http://diverseeducation.com/article/53664

HB 846 *Brown v. Board of Education* Scholarship Program and Fund; created, report. (2004). *Virginia's legislative information system.* https://lis.virginia.gov/cgi-bin/legp604.exe?041+mbr+HB846

Heaton, P. (2008). Childhood educational disruption and later life outcomes: Evidence from Prince Edward County. *Journal of Human Capital, 2*(2), 154–187. http://doi.org/10.2139/ssrn.1091305

Hicks, T., & Pitre, A. (2010). *The educational lockout of Blacks.* University Press of America.

House Joint Resolution, no. 613. (2003). Virginia Department of Education. http://www.doe.virginia.gov/administrators/superintendents_memos/2003/infl05a.pdf

Mason, J. (2002). *Qualitative researching* (2nd ed.). Sage.

Matsuda, M. J. (1987). Looking to the bottom: Critical legal studies and reparations. *Harvard Civil Rights - Civil Liberties Law Review, 22,* 323–399.

Maxwell, J. (2005). *Qualitative research design: An interactive approach* (2nd ed.). Sage.

Maxwell, J. (2009). Designing a qualitative study. In L. Bickman & D. J. Rog (Eds.), *The SAGE handbook of applied social research methods* (2nd ed.). Sage. http://doi.org/10.4135/9781483348858

Merriam, S. B. (2009). *Qualitative research: A guide to design and implementation.* Jossey-Bass.

Patterson, J. T. (2001). *Brown v. Board of Education: A civil rights milestone and its troubled legacy.* Oxford University Press.

Patterson, R. L., & Dupree, L. W. (1994). Older adults. In M. Hersen & S. M. Turner (Eds.), *Diagnostic interviewing.* Plenum.

Peeples, E. H. Jr. (1963). *The study of county decisionmakers, Prince Edward County, Virginia.* Master's notes in The Edward H. Peeples Prince Edward County (VA).

Peeples, E. H. Jr. (2004). *Tragedy of public schools: Prince Edward County, Virginia: A report for the Virginia Advisory Committee to the United States Commission on Civil Rights.* Part 3, postscript by the editor. Virginia Commonwealth Digital Library.

Rector and Visitors of the University of Virginia. (2020). *Universities studying slavery. President's commission on slavery and the University.* University of Virginia. http://slavery.virginia.edu/universities-studying-slavery

Roulston, K. (2010). *Reflective interviewing: A guide to theory and practice.* Sage.

Sampson, H. (2004). Navigating the waves: The usefulness of a pilot in qualitative research. *Qualitative Research, 4*(3), 383–402. http://doi.org/10.1177/1468794104047236

Stake, R. E. (2005). Qualitative case studies. In N. K. Denzin & Y. S. Lincoln (Eds.), *The Sage handbook of qualitative research* (3rd ed., pp. 443–466). Sage.

State Council of Higher Education for Virginia. (2014). *Framework for the statewide strategic plan for higher education in Virginia.* Statewide strategic plan for higher education. http://www.schev.edu/schev/StrategicPlan.asp

Stovall, D. O. (2006). Forging community in race and class: Critical race theory and the quest for social justice in education. *Race, Ethnicity and Education, 9*(3), 243–259. http://doi.org/10.1080/13613320600807550

Sweeney, J. R. (Ed.) (2008). *Race, reason, and massive resistance: The diary of David J. Mays, 1954–1959. Politics and culture in the twentieth century South.* The University of Georgia Press.

Title 30. VA General Assembly. (2010). § *30-231.8. Chapter 34.1. Brown v. Board of Education* Scholarship Program and fund: Powers and duties of the committee. https://law.lis.virginia.gov/vacode/title30/chapter34.1/section30-231.8/

Titus, J. (2011). *Brown's battleground: Students, segregationists, and the struggle for justice in Prince Edward County, Virginia.* University of North Carolina Press.

Turner, K. M. (2004). Both victors and victims: Prince Edward County, Virginia, the NAACP, and *Brown. Virginia Law Review, 90,* 1667–1691.

Virginia Division of Legislative Services. (2005). *Brown v. Board of Education* Scholarship Awards Committee. Legislative Record, Virginia. http://dls.virginia.gov/pubs/legisrec/2005/BvBOE1.htm

Walgrave, L. (2011). Investigating the potentials of restorative justice practice. *Washington University Journal of Law and Policy, 36*(9), 91–139.

Walker, M. U. (2006). Restorative justice and reparations. *Journal of Social Philosophy, 37*(3), 377–395. http://doi.org/10.1111/j.1467-9833.2006.00343.x

Wenzel, M., Okimoto, T. G., Feather, N. T., & Platow, M. J. (2008). Retributive and restorative justice. *Law and Human Behavior, 32*(5), 375–389. http://doi.org/10.1037/e633982013-050

Williams, V. L. (2005). Reading, writing, and reparations: Systemic reform of public schools as a matter of justice. *Michigan Journal of Race and Law, 11,* 419–474. http://doi.org/10.2139/ssrn.707702

Woodley, K. (2019). *The road to healing: A civil rights reparation.* NewSouth Books.

Yamamoto, E. K. (1997). Critical race praxis: Race theory and political lawyering practice in post-civil rights America. *Michigan Law Review, 95,* 821–900. http://doi.org/10.2307/1290048

Yamamoto, E. K. (1998). Racial reparations: Japanese American redress and African American claims. *Boston College Third World Law Journal, 19*(1), 476–523.

Yin, R. K. (2009). *Case study research: Design and methods* (4th ed.). Sage.

Zehr, H. (2002). *The little book of restorative justice.* Good Books.

CHAPTER 2

PRINCE EDWARD COUNTY'S ROLE IN *BROWN V. BOARD OF EDUCATION* AND THE BIRTH OF MASSIVE RESISTANCE

Emily Martin Cochran
Georgia Historic Preservation Division, USA

Introduction

Etta Neal, a Prince Edward County, Virginia, native, recalled about her school days in 1959:

> My mother will tell you, I was the biggest crybaby about [not] going to school. She will tell you she had the hardest time getting it in my head why I could not wake up every morning and go to school…. I'd wake up every morning and say "I want to go to school." I'll never forget one day she brought me to the school here, when they had the chains on the doors, and you know, she touched the chains to say, "See, you can't go to school because the doors are locked," and it had to sink into me that, you know, I can't go in there, into the schools (Vrooman, 2014, p. 15).

Ms. Neal was one of 1,700 Black students in Prince Edward County who were shut out of their education for 5 years due to the White county board of supervisors closing all public schools rather than integrate them in 1959. After the 1951 Moton High School student walkout caught White segregationists by surprise, the White segregationist school officials, county officials, politicians, press, and clergy of southside Virginia mounted a widespread and far-reaching campaign to prevent the US Supreme Court from ordering integration of schools. This effort became known as "massive resistance," and it was a model for how segregationists across the South could resist civil rights legislation and court orders. With the Byrd Organization leading the way, these segregationists fought tooth and nail to preserve their tradition of segregation and the "Virginia Way" of genteel discrimination through every legal strategy, legislative tactic, and means of propaganda they could. What they could not do, however, was break the spirit from the student strike, which remained strong for 8 years, and that spirit initiated one of the court cases that led to the pivotal 1954 *Brown v. Board of Education* Supreme Court decision.

Methodologies

In both scholarship and public memory, the story of civil rights in Prince Edward County and the broader southside Virginia region is not widely recognized. Why have historians and public memory largely ignored the pivotal center of civil rights activism in southside Virginia and its broader significance? Why in historical scholarship does Virginia hold a "moderate" reputation for civil rights when there were major instances of violence as well as massive resistance campaigns to integration? In Prince Edward County and across southside Virginia, racial "moderation" did not prevent major demonstrations. Instead, the White social and political elite crafted a well-coordinated effort and narrative—motivated by an ideology heavily influenced by southern paternalism, honor, and Confederate memory—to undermine and suppress African Americans' efforts during the peak years of the Civil Rights Movement to topple Jim Crow and secure racial equality and justice.

The historical narrative of the Prince Edward movement provides an opportunity to examine several historiographical questions, including questions on where and how social change originated. Did momentum come from grassroots organizing (below) or from institutions with legal and social power (above)? Prince Edward County and southside Virginia have several distinctive factors, including a sizable (almost 50%) Black population and a hegemonic White culture that glorified the former Confederacy. This profile of the region also raises questions about how race, gender, and class intersect in this history. As the cultural turn in historiography shows, ideology and culture are factors in prompting protest as well as the backlash to protest. White supremacy was the hegemonic culture in the region, and White elites built up this culture through the public memorialization of the final events of the Civil War. This link to Confederate memorialization brings up questions about the United Daughters of the Confederacy and the role of elite White women in suppressing the local movements.

In understanding the historical landscape of southside Virginia, frameworks set forth by Antonio Gramsci (Forgacs, 2003) and Barbara Fields (1982) offer tools to analyze the connections between the ideological and material histories of civil rights in southside Virginia. To analyze the culture and ideology of the region, Gramsci's theory of cultural hegemony provides an explanation of the dominance of White supremacy and the lost cause of the Confederacy. According to Gramsci, a ruling group uses dominant ideology to maintain politically, socially, and economically social norms and the status quo. This dominant ideology is framed in sacred terms, usually, and used to justify the status quo as natural, traditional, and normal. Gramsci also called historical actors who mediate or resist hegemony "intellectuals"; traditional intellectuals maintain the status quo, while organic intellectuals come from the working class and develop class consciousness to create a mass movement. As Barbara Ransby noted in her biography of civil rights leader Ella Baker, Baker was a Gramscian "organic intellectual" (Ransby, 2003, p. 6); Baker believed change came from within communities (Ransby, 2003). This style of leadership was true for Prince Edward County, as illustrated in the records of the National Association for the Advancement of Colored People (NAACP) and oral histories of the students who participated in the student strike and resulting court case.

Barbara Fields's (1982) framework on race is also helpful in understanding how White supremacy became embedded in southside Virginia's culture. She argued that race is a "notion that is profoundly and in its very essence ideological" (p. 144). She was careful to note, however, that while race is an ideological notion, it is something that is very real, as it is the "embodiment of thought of real social relations" (p. 151). Fields also noted that race "becomes the ideological medium through which Americans confronted questions of sovereignty and power" (p. 168) and that race holds power over historical narratives because of deep scars left on society from the unraveling of slavery. This is reflected in how the "Virginia Way" institutionalized White supremacy in southside.

The historical evidence in the papers of leading White segregationists—including Senator Harry Byrd, congressman and former governor William M. Tuck, and newspaper editor James J. Kilpatrick—illustrated how racist ideology translated into concrete, actionable plans to prevent racial integration in not only Virginia but also across the South and the nation.

Review of Literature

The historical literature on the Civil Rights Movement has grown exponentially in the last few decades, but little scholarship exists on the whole of the movement in Virginia. The peak decades of the Civil Rights Movement in Virginia can be categorized into three stages: school integration and the White pushback (termed "massive resistance") of the 1950s, the sit-in movement of the early 1960s, and incorporation into the national Civil Rights Movement in the mid-1960s. Most historical scholarship on the Civil Rights Movement in Virginia begins with massive resistance and emphasizes the White response to school integration and focuses on the conservative politics of civil rights. Historical literature on the last two stages of the movement in Virginia is still emerging, but there are many personal accounts and monographs that deal with the movement from a national standpoint; these accounts mention Virginia briefly. The most recent works focus on the closure of Prince Edward County Public Schools and the role of the NAACP in Virginia.

Most of the historiography of the Virginia Civil Rights Movement focuses on the period of massive resistance, the White refusal to integrate schools after the *Brown v. Board of Education* decision led by the political machine of Governor Harry Byrd. The earliest works (starting in the 1960s) on massive resistance use narrative to describe the birth of massive resistance as instituted by the politicians tied to the Byrd political machine, whom most historians depict as White supremacists (Muse, 1961; Smith, 1965; Wilkinson, 1968). Other scholars during this period also argued that White moderates were mostly silent on the matter of desegregation. More recent books have expanded the focus on White moderate responses to massive resistance (Lassiter & Lewis, 1998; Leidholdt, 1997).[1]

While the historiography of Virginia's massive resistance covers White responses to civil rights activity thoroughly, the most recent scholarship provides a well-developed Black perspective. Brian Daugherity's (2016) *Keep on Keeping On: The NAACP and the Implementation of Brown v. Board of Education in Virginia* argued that the Virginia State Conference of the NAACP was instrumental in implementing integration amid the White-led massive resistance because of its hierarchical structure as well as its proximity to the NAACP's national headquarters in New York and Howard University in Washington, DC, a training ground for Black lawyers. Other scholars of the closing of Prince Edward County schools, including Christopher Bonastia (2012) and Jill Titus (2011), also argue that the local Farmville movement was unique in many ways, but not incomprehensible in the broader scholarship, and therefore deserves a closer look. Another useful work is Larissa Smith Fergeson's (2001) dissertation, "Where the South Begins: Black Politics and Civil Rights Activism in Virginia, 1930–1951." Fergeson's dissertation provided historical context for Black activism in Virginia and the grassroots organizing that let the movement explode in the 1950s and 1960s.

By 1963, the Virginia movements (including the movements in southside) became part of the national movement led by the national organizations, including the Southern Christian Leadership Conference and Student Nonviolent Coordinating Committee, incorporating them into their own projects. Broader scholarship has argued about the effectiveness of each group's tactics. However, scholarly work on this period of Virginia's Civil Rights Movement has only just been emerging. Simon Hall (2007), Brian Lee (2015), as well as Lee and Brian Daugherity (2013) argued that many Black Virginians found the NAACP's tactics too conservative and wanted to adopt the more radical techniques of the Student Nonviolent Coordinating Committee and Southern Christian Leadership Conference. Brian Lee's (2015) dissertation also shed light on how the federal government intervened in civil rights activity in Virginia by tracing the Kennedy administration's involvement. However, the Southern Christian Leadership Conference prioritized the Deep South movement over Virginia, because Virginia was considered more "moderate" than the Deep South states, where White resistance was seemingly more vicious. Amid the lack of scholarship, these pieces have provided a starting point for further research in this area (Hall, 2007; Lee & Daugherity, 2013).

The Prince Edward County and other significant movements in southside Virginia do not fit neatly into the standard narrative that the Virginia Civil Rights Movement was moderate, focusing mainly on massive resistance. Historians began documenting and crafting the story of the direct-action protest in Farmville, which is not well-known even in local history, within the last 15 years. Recent efforts to collect oral histories from Black student participants and local leaders resulted in a rich narrative of events of the movement. During the movement, these events were originally documented by the local and federal court case files and local media reports, which only gave the White perspective of the events. These additional sources, when combined with memoirs and records from movement leaders and organizations, tell a story of Black student-initiated protest supported by local Black professionals that used legal means and direct-action protest to advocate for equality. They help make a case that, while the southside movements may have had a reputation of failure, there was progress (Kelley, 2010).[2] By documenting Black activism and recovering the thoughts and perspectives of African Americans who led and participated in the southside movements, this work argues that the southside movements created real change and brought progress, which challenges the traditional interpretation that they "failed."

In the 20th century, southside Virginia was a racially repressive place. White elites maintained segregation and discrimination through the

"Virginia Way" (patronage at the highest level of politics in the state and also the genteel way of dealing with political and class conflict). The fruit of this mindset is evident in southside Virginia in how White segregationist politicians responded to labor organizing and civil rights activities. The White political elite used tradition, public memory, and history as a weapon to keep Black citizens of southside "in their place," but elites did not hesitate to use violence to suppress organizing.

Grassroots activism defined the Virginia movements, but assistance from national civil rights organizations and the goal of federal interventions helped galvanize momentum at the local level. Initial challenges to the Virginia Way came from Black students' grassroots activism, but in working with the state-level and national-level civil rights organizations, they pooled resources to keep the local movements alive in the face of repression. Black citizens faced an uphill battle against the Virginia Way, but they also recognized the power of the federal government to intervene on their behalf.

The backlash to civil rights activity in southside cannot be perceived as "moderate." The Virginia Way only had a veneer of gentility because when Black students challenged the norms of southside, Whites used police repression, violence, and other methods to keep norms of segregation firmly in place. Closing public schools for everyone for 5 years and responding to peaceful protests with billy clubs is not moderate.

The movements in southside illustrate the power of networks within the Civil Rights Movement and the resistance to it. The two local movements in southside demonstrate the power of the Byrd machine's orchestrated network. They also show the communication of Black activists across the region and the development of tactics that would help liberate other locales across the Deep South—constantly learning from other movements. The Virginia Way was often characterized as less overt and extreme than tactics used in the Deep South, but the politicians and propagators of the way communicated with groups across the Deep South to resist desegregation in all forms.

The story of civil rights in southside Virginia belongs in large part to the Black students of the region. In 1951, students—led by 16-year-old Barbara Johns—decided they had enough of segregated and inferior schools. A younger generation rose up—not content with the status quo of Virginia. Their initiative galvanized progressive Black leaders in the county to organize to make a formal challenge to the unequal conditions of schools. The White leadership of Prince Edward County dug in their heels and took the case all the way to the Supreme Court. But once the Supreme Court told them they had to integrate schools and change their "way of life," all bets were off. Rather than comply with the Supreme Court ruling, Prince Edward closed down their public school system in 1959.

Davis v. Prince Edward County School Board and the Road to Brown

The 1951 student walkout at Moton High School in Farmville, Virginia, galvanized the local African American community to make a legal challenge to the blatant discrimination in the public county schools. The students, with assistance from the NAACP, rallied their parents to file a lawsuit asking for the desegregation of the county schools. While their initial goal was equalization of school facilities, they recognized that the NAACP would be most helpful if they became a test case for K–12 integration. The students and parents bravely signed a petition to the county asking for desegregation, knowing the risks of retaliation by the White community and their White employers. When the school board refused to act, the petition officially became the lawsuit *Davis v. Prince Edward County School Board*. This case wound its way through the US District Court, the US Court of Appeals, and finally to the Supreme Court, and after 2 years, it became part of the combined school-integration suit *Brown v. Board of Education of Topeka*. Joining four other integration suits from around the country, *Davis v. Prince Edward County School Board* set a new course for the nascent Civil Rights Movement nationally and also triggered one of the strongest instances of White backlash to civil rights in the 20th century, exemplified by the actions of the White power structure and at-large White community in southside Virginia.

While the progression from planning the student walkout in April 1951 to filing the suit for integration in May 1951 happened at lightning speed, the progression of *Davis v. Prince Edward County School Board* took 3 years before the Supreme Court made its final ruling—many of the students who led the walkout and strike graduated from Moton before the case finished. From the filing of *Davis* on May 21, 1951, to opening arguments in February 1952, very little happened in Prince Edward County to indicate that its African American community was leading an effort to overthrow Jim Crow segregation. However, the White leaders of Prince Edward County began their campaign of intimidation to punish the adults who assisted the community in filing the suit in July 1951. The county school board voted to not renew the contract of M. Boyd Jones, principal of Moton High School, and Rev. L. Francis Griffin faced efforts to remove him from the pastorate of First Baptist Church in Farmville. In response to this effort, which came from outside of his congregation, he delivered a sermon on July 28 titled "The Prophecy of Equalization," and boldly declared from the pulpit that their cause of desegregation was just and that no matter the cost, they would stay the course:

> But we all may rest assured whatever else might be said, God does not believe in segregation.... When is it that every Southern church and clergymen will

proclaim the "accepted year of the Lord?" When shall men clamor for brotherhood and there shall be no man bound to the chains of circumstances? When can every citizen look to his leadership with veneration and respect? How long, Lord, how long? ... Of course, there are those who will cry that if you do not like the South, MOVE! How silly! There is no record which says you can solve a problem by running away from it (Griffin, 1951, cited in Daugherity & Grogan, 2019, pp. 52–53).

Reverend Griffin and the Black community of Prince Edward County had no intention of running from those who would try to intimidate them, but they would have to wait for some time to see movement on their case.

Arguments for *Davis v. County School Board of Prince Edward County* opened in US District Court on February 25, 1952. NAACP lawyers Oliver Hill, Spottswood Robinson, and Robert Carter represented the plaintiffs, while T. Justin Moore, Archibald Robertson, and T. Justin Moore Jr. represented Prince Edward County; and J. Lindsay Almond, the Virginia attorney general, and Henry Wickham, the assistant attorney general, represented the Commonwealth of Virginia in aid to the defense. A three-judge panel made up of judges Archibald Dobie, Sterling Hutcheson, and Albert Vickers Bryan heard the case. In US District Court, the plaintiffs laid out the disparities of the Black and White schools of Prince Edward County, arguing that the disparities were a violation of the equal protection clause in the 14th Amendment. The plaintiffs did request if the court did not rule to eliminate segregation, that the court require the county to equalize the schools. In the suit, the plaintiffs specifically challenged section 140 of the Constitution of Virginia—which stated, "White and colored children shall not be taught in the same school"—as a breach of the 14th Amendment and the Civil Rights Act of 1876. Throughout the hearings, expert witnesses testified to the degree that segregation damaged Black children's development and educational attainment. The defense called expert witnesses to counter the plaintiffs' evidence, including the president of the University of Virginia, Colgate Darden. From the trial transcripts, the counsels for the defense and even Judge Dobie were hostile, condescending, and rude to the witnesses for the plaintiffs and plaintiffs' counsel. Moore Sr., Robertson, and Judge Dobie were all considered paragons of Virginia's genteel society, but their actions in the trial revealed how defensive that gentility was of its segregated society and norms (Kluger, 2004, Chapter 20).

Not surprisingly, the panel ruled against the plaintiffs, stating in the opinion, "Separation of White and colored 'children' in the public schools of Virginia has for generations been a part of the mores of her people. To have separate schools has been their use and wont" (*Davis v. County School Board*). The panel did rule that the public school facilities were unequal and ordered the county immediately "to pursue with diligence and dispatch their present program, now afoot and progressing, to replace the Moton buildings and facilities with a new building and new equipment, or otherwise remove the inequality in them" (*Davis v. County School Board*).

The Prince Edward County officials redoubled their efforts to move quickly on a new Moton High School, which they began in response to the filing of the suit in June 1951. They borrowed the strategy of segregationists in South Carolina, who moved quickly to preempt any court orders to desegregate in response to the *Briggs v. Elliott* school desegregation case from Clarendon County, South Carolina. A similar case in many regards to *Davis*, *Briggs* came 1 year before the Prince Edward County suit. NAACP lawyers who worked on the *Davis* suit, including Robert Carter and Spottswood Robinson, along with Thurgood Marshall argued that the Clarendon County Black schools were inferior to the White schools. Surprising the NAACP lawyers, the counsel for the defense, Robert Figg, conceded in court that the schools were unequal and pledged that Clarendon County would equalize the schools. That panel ruled 2-1, and the dissenting judge, J. Waties Waring, wrote the first dissent against segregation, stating that "segregation is per se inequality." While the *Briggs* plaintiffs also appealed their case to the Supreme Court, the Clarendon County school officials moved quickly to work with South Carolina governor James Byrnes and the General Assembly to pass legislation to fund a "equalization" program in South Carolina through levying a 3% sales tax that yielded $75 million. As construction began on Black schools in South Carolina, these politicians made clear that they would not yield to the courts. Speaking in March 1951 to the South Carolina Educational Association at the same time the *Davis* case was in the US District Court, Governor Byrnes stated that the purpose of the school building program was to maintain segregation and prevent federally ordered integration ("November 26, 1952—School Desegregation Cases," 1981). While the Commonwealth of Virginia did not take up a building plan like that of South Carolina across the state, the officials of Prince Edward County moved swiftly to complete a new Moton High School. The "equalized" Moton opened in September 1953, while the *Davis* case continued in the courts.

The NAACP appealed *Davis* to the Supreme Court in July 1952, and its lawyers began making plans to argue it along with concurring school integration cases, including *Briggs v. Elliott*, *Brown v. Board of Education* out of Kansas, *Bolling v. Sharpe* from Washington, DC, and *Gebhart v. Belton* from Delaware. While *Briggs* reached the Supreme Court first, it was remanded to district court in January 1952 for a hearing on the progress of equalizing schools in Clarendon County. The district court ruled just a few days after the *Davis* case that the equalization attempts would suffice. This decision left *Brown* the only case on the Supreme Court's docket in 1952, so when the appeals from *Davis*, *Briggs*, *Bolling*, and *Gebhart* also made it to the Supreme Court in the summer and fall of 1952, the Supreme Court justices voted to combine the cases for a hearing on December 9, 1952 (Kluger, 2004, pp. 540–542). The Supreme Court then waited another year for a second round of arguments in December 1953 that focused on the question of the intent of the 14th Amendment's equal protection clause. In this hearing, Thurgood Marshall and Spottswood Robinson argued the Southern cases of *Briggs* and *Davis*, facing off against prior opponents T. Justin Moore and J. Lindsay Almond, and lawyer John W. Davis, retained by the states of South Carolina and Virginia to argue the appellants' case ("School Segregation Cases—Order of Argument Record Group 267", 1953). The Court deliberated for several more months, but on May 17, 1954, it unanimously overturned *Plessy v. Ferguson* in its ruling that segregation in public schools was unconstitutional.

Initial responses to the Warren court's opinion in Virginia ranged from jubilation to despair. The NAACP lawyers rejoiced at the decision and the language in the opinion, which struck a major blow to the entire system of Jim Crow in the South; Moton student leader John Stokes recounted with pride that of the five cases in the decision, the *Davis* suit was the only one that was student-led, and that case was "only the first step in overturning segregation in America" (Stokes, 2007, p. 111; Sullivan, 2009, p. 420). Virginia's segregationist politicians were less thrilled, to severely understate it. In the initial statements from Harry Byrd, Governor Thomas Stanley, and former governor Bill Tuck, we see the seeds of massive resistance already fomenting in their minds. Senator Byrd's statement from the same day as the ruling recognized the gravity of the situation, as this ruling threatened to upend the Virginia Way; he stated that the decision was "the most serious blow that has yet been struck against the rights of the states in a matter vitally affecting their authority and welfare" (Byrd, 1954). Byrd immediately positioned the South as the victim in this ruling, implying that the federal government was imposing a hardship on the South when southern governments had complied with what the law of the land said. Finally, Byrd predicted that southerners would not accept this ruling, and that it would be deleterious to the education of children (Byrd, 1954).

Freshman congressman Bill Tuck of Virginia's fifth district agreed with Byrd, stating,

> The decision imposes on the good people of America a way of life not envisioned in our Constitution and to which many are unalterably unopposed …. The abolishment of segregation in our schools will lower the standards of public education, and will tend to mar the cordial and understanding race relations which have existed for so long (Crawley, 1978, p. 220).

Tuck was much more colorful in his description of the Warren Court in private letters, calling them "nine reprehensible individuals gasconading in judicial ermine" (Crawley, 1978, p. 223). The governor of Virginia, Thomas Stanley, called for "cooler heads to prevail," and announced he would form a biracial commission to study the issue, but this statement was really a stopgap while the segregationists planned a response to the *Brown* ruling. Politicians across southside, including now Congressman Tuck, began hatching plans to resist this order as long as they could.

Southside's White Backlash to the *Brown* Decision and the Creation of Massive Resistance

As state politicians recovered from the shock of the *Brown* decision, southside segregationists began organizing to do all that they could to stop the integration of schools. Their efforts to resist court-ordered integration became a model for segregationists across the South, broadening the larger "massive resistance" to integration. Leading figures in southside, namely Prince Edward County and neighboring counties, began meeting at a firehouse in Petersburg to create an organization that would function like the NAACP on the behalf of the segregationists of southside. *Farmville Herald* editor J. Barrye Wall and congressman Watkins Abbitt of Virginia's fourth district—which included Nottoway, Appomattox, and much of the Black belt counties in the Tidewater region—were among this leadership. Congressman Bill Tuck also participated in these organizational meetings. The group they officially organized on October 26, 1954, became known as the Defenders of State Sovereignty and Individual Liberties. The name was suggested by Wall, who drew the name from a Confederate memorial close to his newspaper's office (Daugherity & Grogan, 2019, p. 99). While on the surface their purpose seemed respectable, they were in many ways the Virginian counterpart of the White citizens' councils founded in Mississippi on July 11, 1954. From the stated purpose of the group, the organization pledged to "employ every lawful means to defend and perpetuate them [the right to determine segregation of the races], to the end that this Republic may continue and prosper" ("For State Sovereignty and Individual Liberties," 1955). The group elected Farmville natives to leadership positions, including Robert Crawford, chairman of the Prince Edward County school board, as the president of the organization ("For State Sovereignty and Individual Liberties," 1955). The Defenders quickly went to work to influence the commission that Governor Stanley organized in August 1954. This commission—led by state senator Garland Gray, a founding member of the Defenders—set out to study the *Brown* decision and make recommendations for education policy. The Defenders set out to make a "Plan for Virginia," and when the Gray Commission released its findings in November 1955, the recommendations were the ones the Defenders had approved.

The other priority of the Defenders at the time was to recruit as many as possible into their membership. The 18 founding members quickly established chapters all over Virginia. Bill Tuck's home county of Halifax created the largest chapter (Crawley, 1978, p. 227). As the chapters grew, the Defenders became more extreme in their rhetoric. Tuck and the Defenders legal counsel, Collins Denny Jr., spoke at a rally packed into the Halifax County High School gymnasium in November 1955 and declared the White supremacist beliefs of the Defenders, as previously mentioned. Denny went on to also laud the resistance that Prince Edward County and Clarendon County, South Carolina, mounted:

> Prince Edward was under the gun but Prince Edward rose on her hind feet and said she would appropriate no money for integrated schools. If it had not been for Prince Edward County and Clarendon County, S.C. standing alone at the moment we would have court decrees all over Virginia and the South ordering school integration ("South Boston Rally Draws 2,300 Crowd," 1955).

This reference to South Carolina in Denny's speech was not just a rhetorical device; the Defenders were coordinating with the White citizens' councils of South Carolina, Mississippi, and other Deep South states. A report on the "New Ku Klux Klan" by the national NAACP office and a report from Herbert Mitchell (1955/1981) of the National Agricultural Workers Union to the American Federation of Labor and Congress of Industrial Organizations characterized the Defenders' activity as part of the White backlash and terrorism happening across the South (Geyer, 1955/1981).

A month later, in December 1955, there was a mass meeting of segregationists and White supremacist organizations in Memphis, Tennessee, though it was organized in secret. Delegates from 12 Southern states went to Memphis to organize a national effort to "to fight racial integration and other efforts to destroy the Constitution." Leading Southern politicians were in attendance, including Senator James Eastland, Senator Strom Thurmond, Governor Marvin Griffin of Georgia, future senator Herman Talmadge of Georgia, Fielding Wright of Mississippi (who ran as Thurmond's vice presidential choice on the 1948 states' rights ticket), and southside Virginia's own Bill Tuck, Watkins Abbitt, attorney James S. Easley of South Boston, and J. Segar Gravatt of Blackstone, who was also the legal counsel for the Prince Edward County School Board. Also of note, South Carolina sent S. E. Rogers of Summerton as part of their delegation to represent the interest of Clarendon County. Naming themselves the "Federation for Constitutional Government," this group would serve as a channel of communication among the state groups, including the Defenders and the White citizens' councils. While at the Memphis meeting, the federation participants swapped tactics in resisting the court order, including economic boycott and reprisals and adopting the doctrine of interposition to "nullify and void Supreme Court decision in the racial area," an idea from the Defenders in Virginia. In the keynote address, James Eastland of Mississippi said the purpose of this federation would be to

... mobilize and organize public opinion.... We are about to embark on a great crusade, a crusade to restore Americanism and return the control of our Government to our people. In addition our organization will carry on its banner the slogan of free enterprise, and we will fight those organizations who attempt with much success to socialize industry and the great medical profession of this country (Lewis, 1955).

Chairman of the executive committee of the federation, John Barr of Louisiana, raised the stakes further in his comments:

Defeat means death, the death of Southern culture and our aspirations as an Anglo-Saxon people. Generations of Southerners yet unborn will cherish our memory because they will realize that the fight we now wage will have preserved for them their untainted racial heritage, their culture, and the institutions of the Anglo-Saxon race (Lewis, 1955).

After this meeting, the Defenders continued to work to grow their chapters, exert their influences on state policy, and coordinate with groups across the South.

After the 1954 *Brown* decision, Virginia's state officials began laying the groundwork for what would become its official policy of "massive resistance." First, Governor Stanley issued a public statement that "admonished citizens to receive the decision with cool heads and sane minds," and he also considered creating a biracial commission made up of educational leaders from across the commonwealth ("Virginia Since May 17, 1954," 1981). But on June 25, 1954, the governor took a hard line against the ruling and stated that he would use all legal means to continue segregated schools in Virginia. He turned the reins of the legal implementation over to Virginia's attorney general, J. Lindsay Almond, who helped the southside counties pass resolutions that vowed to maintain segregated schools. Tuck's home county of Halifax was the first to do so on June 8, and 55 counties passed similar resolutions ("Virginia Since May 17, 1954," 1981). At the end of the summer on August 30, Governor Stanley appointed the Gray Commission, made up of representatives from southside. With these actions, the Virginia State Conference of the NAACP noted that the opposition to the Supreme Court ruling mainly stemmed from three interrelated areas—the Gray Commission itself, members of the General Assembly and county boards of supervisors, and the Defenders. What the NAACP did not note was that these groups were one and the same, so making this coordinated effort against desegregation was relatively easy and showed how much of a grip the southside segregationists held over the state government ("Virginia Since May 17, 1954," 1981).

From the summer of 1954 through the end of 1956, the segregationist politicians, government officials, lawyers, newspaper editors, the United

Daughters of the Confederacy, and the Sons of Confederate Veterans all communicated with each other and other like-minded individuals across the South to put into place a plan to legally resist the *Brown* ruling. Senator Harry Byrd held the highest political influence of the group, and just about every southside official, state official, and newspaper editor of the region sought out his opinion in every decision. Senator Byrd remained focused on what he could do in Congress, but people like Congressman Bill Tuck kept him apprized of who was running for political office in these districts because Byrd was still the giant in the organization—his approval guaranteed election. Byrd also coordinated the most with state officials, including Lindsay Almond, but Richmond newspaper editor James Kilpatrick editor of the *Richmond News Leader,* cast the widest net of influence, as he corresponded with newspaper editors across the South, the citizens councils of Mississippi, the United Daughters of the Confederacy's national office, and other officials, including judges from all over Virginia. He often wrote to J. Segar Gravatt, and they together hammered out the proposals that the Defenders offered the Gray Commission. Most of the correspondence Kilpatrick, Gravatt, and Byrd wrote dealt with major themes of (1) calling a constitutional convention to amend the state Constitution's requirement of public schools, (2) the doctrine of interposition, and (3) the creation and funding of a private school system (*Papers of Harry Flood Byrd; Papers of James Kilpatrick; Papers of J. Segar Gravatt*).

With the founding of the Gray Commission in 1954, Virginia's state legislators set out to find a way to keep schools segregated legally. In their January 1955 progress report, it was clear that the commission was not interested in finding an alternative to massive resistance: "After careful consideration, our conclusions indicate that the vast majority of Virginia Citizens (both White and colored) favor the retention of racially segregated public education" ("Virginia Since May 17, 1954," 1981). The commission issued its final report on November 11, 1955, with the following recommendations:

> 1) Some integration be permitted in some areas, 2) no student (White or colored) will be forced to attend an integrated school, 3) a special session of the General Assembly to be called to (a) authorize enabling legislation to hold Constitutional Convention (b) Enact the recommendations of the Gray report, 4) Section 141 of State Constitution be deleted by Constitutional Convention action, 5) adoption of pupil assignment plan, and 6) payment of tuition grants to those parents who are not willing to send their children to integrated schools or where public schools have been abolished ("Virginia Since May 17, 1954," 1981).

Of the six recommendations, the Defenders had proposed two of them—the revising of the state constitution through a constitutional convention to eliminate public schools and the authorization of tuition grants (Defenders of State Sovereignty and Individual Liberties, 1955).

The commonwealth moved quickly to start the process through the calling of a referendum vote that would call for a constitutional convention. Bill Tuck and Watkins Abbitt proposed the referendum before the Gray Commission made their recommendations public, but the proposal received a hearty endorsement from Senator Byrd:

> I am very much interested in the Tuck-Abbitt proposal for the referendum in the localities on the question of enforced integration in our public schools.... Such referendums on the local level would in no way conflict with the Supreme Court decision ("Statement by Senator Harry Flood Byrd for release in morning papers of Tuesday, November 1, 1955," 1955).

A few weeks later, Governor Stanley called for a special session of the General Assembly on November 30, and the body authorized a referendum vote for January 9, 1956. The Byrd Organization, the Defenders, and White segregationists immediately began their campaign to stump for voting "yes" for the convention. Senator Byrd compared the situation to a serious crisis, "like that of the War Between the States." He encouraged the General Assembly to act "with wisdom and high patriotism" ("Statement by Senator Harry F. Byrd on the Referendum to be held on January 9, 1956," 1955).

Conversely, the Virginia State Conference of the NAACP also moved swiftly to oppose the referendum vote. E. B. Henderson (1981), president of the Virginia State Conference, issued a statement denouncing the vote as an attempt to weaken the public school system by those who were "less literate and prejudiced."

The official wording of the referendum vote made it clear that the commonwealth intended to abolish public education. The vote explained that the convention's stated purpose was

> ... to change Section 141 of the present Constitution, so that state and local funds may be used in the future for tuition grants to children who elect to attend private non-sectarian schools. The declared purpose of this amendment is to permit localities to substitute private education for public, if they so decide, and/or to require communities that integrate their schools to divide their financial resources between public education and grants to children who prefer to enroll in private schools ("Statement by the Northern Virginia Unit of the Washington Ethical Society," 1956/1981).

While the Black community tried to convince voters to vote against it through its own ad campaign, the referendum had the support of the governor, the Byrd Organization, and the majority of the state legislature ("The Gray Amendment and the Public School System of Virginia," 1956/1981). The vote passed 2-1. Roy Wilkins of the national NAACP released a statement after the vote that the NAACP was prepared to meet any move that the state made to evade integration ("NAACP Is Prepared to Test Bid," 1955/1981).

While Virginia made plans to implement the convention, the General Assembly took up legislation in its regular session to further delay action on integration in schools, including the doctrine of state sovereignty and interposition. Interposition is a legal theory that dates back to the nullification crisis of the antebellum period, in which a state could interpose its sovereignty between the people and the federal government. Virginia's brand of interposition was an attempt to "nullify" the Supreme Court decision through forcing a constitutional amendment through Congress that would make segregated schools illegal; when the amendment went to the states for ratification, it would fail to meet the threshold required for ratification, and in the segregationists' view, this failure would then render the *Brown* decision void, as the American public had rejected it through the process of amending the Constitution. This scheme was first proposed by James Kilpatrick and discussed and championed at the December 1955 Memphis meeting of segregationists. It gained hearty approval there and led to other Southern states introducing similar proposals, although several of these states implied in their resolutions that interposition gave the states the right to nullify certain laws (Lewis, 1955; Reid, 1956, p. 111). Legal scholars of the time agreed that the doctrine of interposition (and the doctrines of nullification and secession) held no legal basis because of the adoption of the 14th Amendment and because the Civil War repudiated secession, nullification, and interposition (Reid, 1956, p. 116). However, the interposition resolutions offered a political stand on which to build massive resistance. Along with the interposition resolution, the General Assembly passed in the same session a bill that penalized Arlington County for announcing their gradual integration plan by abolishing the method of a popularly elected school board. Other bills included one that withheld all state monies from counties that integrated schools and one that barred federal employees from serving in local municipal jobs (targeting Arlington County). The General Assembly also passed a resolution that declared that Virginia would operate segregated public schools during 1956–1957 ("Virginia Since May 17, 1954," 1981).

Coming on the heels of this action from the General Assembly, Harry Byrd took Virginia's nascent massive resistance plan national in an interview on February 26, 1956. In a statement from his office to the press, Senator Byrd said,

> If we can organize the Southern States for massive resistance to this order I think that in time the rest of the country will realize that racial integration is not going to be accepted in the South.... In interposition, the South has a perfectly legal means of appeal from the Supreme Court's order ("Byrd Calls on South to Challenge Court," 1956, cited in Daugherity & Grogan, 2019, p. 84).

This statement also foreshadowed the forthcoming "Southern Manifesto" that 18 senators sponsored. Two weeks later on March 12, Senator Walter George of Georgia and Rep. Howard W. Smith of Virginia presented the "Southern Manifesto" to Congress. Officially titled "Declaration of Constitutional Principles," Southern members of Congress pledged to "use all lawful means to bring about a reversal of this decision which is contrary to the Constitution and to prevent the use of force in its implementation." Ten members of the House representing Virginia signed it along with Senators Byrd and A. Willis Robertson. The House members included Edward J. Robeson Jr., Porter Hardy Jr., J. Vaughan Gary, Watkins M. Abbitt, William M. Tuck, Richard H. Poff, Burr P. Harrison, Howard W. Smith, W. Pat Jennings, and Joel T. Broyhill, representing all of Virginia's congressional districts ("Declaration of Constitutional Principles," 1956). Virginia led the way for the South to take its stand against integration, and through the spring and summer of 1956, the General Assembly rolled out even more legislation to prevent the integration of schools across the state.

In July 1956, Governor Stanley wrote the Gray Commission's executive committee to announce his program of massive resistance. He agreed largely with the November 1955 report but would not endorse the pupil assignment plan as that would "accept the principles of integration of the races in public schools" (Stanley, 1956/1981). Stanley also intended to introduce legislation that would give the governor power to withhold money from schools on his discretion. One month later, Stanley announced his package of legislation to the general public, along with a proposal to amend the state's statute on a prohibition against solicitation, running, and capping, and a revisal to the provisions for disbarment of attorneys, both aimed at crippling the NAACP's legal efforts in Virginia ("Virginia Since May 17, 1954," 1981). In September 1956, the General Assembly passed a law requiring any public school under a court order to desegregate to close. This law came to fruition 2 years later in September 1958 when the localities of Norfolk, Charlottesville, and Warren County closed their schools, leaving nearly 13,000 children out of school. These districts were under court-ordered integration, and the newly elected Governor J. Lindsay Almond closed those schools. The courts, both the Virginia Supreme Court and US District Court, struck down the laws that required the closing in January 1959, and in February 1959, the schools in Norfolk began reopening, and Arlington began desegregating schools (Eskridge, 2021). This attempt of closing schools by Governor Almond was the only statewide attempt to shut down public schools, but it gave a model for Prince Edward County, whose officials kept searching for ways to stave off integration.

After the ruling on May 17, 1954, Prince Edward County moved quickly to formulate a plan to keep the federal courts at bay and defend segregation.

On May 21, the *Farmville Herald* published an editorial calling for the county to solve this problem before the court made them:

> Since Prince Edward County is one of the principals in this decision, it is to be expected that more attention will be focused upon it. As we have pointed out before, some national organizations, the press, and possibly other phases of communication seeking the sensational may attempt to find 'grist for the mill' in our community. The problem is ours, we must solve it! Unfortunately, our county was made a principal in this momentous suit. It came about because we failed to seek a solution of our own...Future relations and a solution to the grave problem confronting us depends on our ability to think clearly and logically. This newspaper continues its firm belief in the principles of segregation in public schools in Southside Virginia, and hopes that a plan can be formulated to continue development of the schools on a segregated basis, within the framework of the decision (*Farmville Herald*, 1954).

The first plan the county implemented originated in South Carolina—equalization of the segregated schools. As *Davis* moved through the courts, Prince Edward County school officials moved immediately on securing a location for a new Moton High School, and by September 1953, classes began at the new location (Daugherity & Grogan, 2019, p. xvii). After the *Brown* decision, the Prince Edward County board of supervisors, like other southside counties, passed a resolution that it would never operate integrated schools. This five-point resolution stated that (1) Prince Edward County was "unalterably opposed" to integration, (2) integration would be impossible, (3) the board was willing to use its powers to continue segregated schools, (4) all officials of the commonwealth should do likewise, and (5) a copy of this resolution was to go to the governor, attorney general, state senators, and delegates in the House (Prince Edward County Board of Supervisors, 1954, cited in Daugherity & Grogan, 2019). Around the same time, future members of the Defenders of State Sovereignty and Individual Liberties began organizing in Farmville, including Robert Crawford and J. Barrye Wall (Daugherity & Grogan, 2019, p. xvii).

For 1 year, it seemed as if ignoring the court decision would be enough, but when the Supreme Court handed down a second ruling, known as the *Brown II* decision, the White segregationists in Prince Edward County sprang into action. Led by Robert Crawford, parents and school officials organized the Prince Edward School Foundation to lay the groundwork for developing a private school on June 7, 1955, at a mass meeting sponsored by the Defenders. Held at Longwood College, this meeting resulted in the formal creation of the school foundation to raise money for the private school system. The organizers presented a motion to guarantee the salaries of current White teachers in the public schools; this motion passed with an overwhelming majority. A second motion was introduced to pay for the salaries of all current Black teachers in the public schools; this motion was vehemently opposed. With these marching orders, White segregationist politicians began a massive fundraizing campaign for the potential private school system in Prince Edward County if they were forced to close schools. A month later, a federal three-judge panel ruled that the county could have 1 more year of grace to desegregate schools (Rorty, 1956, cited in Daugherity & Grogan, 2019). With this deadline, county officials began taking more extreme stances.

Closing Public Schools in Prince Edward County

In May 1956, Prince Edward's board of supervisors began going down the road of school closures. On May 3, the board of supervisors stated it would not appropriate any money for desegregated schools. That summer, the Stanley plan for massive resistance passed, buying the county a little more time while the NAACP filed another suit, *Allen v. County School Board of Prince Edward County*, to challenge the extra delay. The case was argued in US District Court in July 1958. Coming a year after the violent desegregation of Central High School in Little Rock, Arkansas, Judge Sterling Hutcheson ruled in this case that due to witnesses' testimonies, integration should be delayed for 7 more years. These witnesses were Sheriff James T. Clark, school board members Lester E. Andrews, B. Calvin Bass, commissioner of revenue D. C. Womack, and school superintendent T. J. McIlwaine. According to Judge Hutchinson, the witnesses testified that

> ... racial relations in the County have deteriorated to a marked degree since 1954. They believe that the effectiveness of the entire educational system in the County is suffering as a result of the atmosphere in which the schools are being operated. They express apprehension with respect to both violence and closing of the schools if the motion of the plaintiffs should be granted. The Sheriff pointed to the necessity of maintaining order in the County having an area of 354 square miles, bisected by highways over which school buses travel. It is his opinion that the local enforcement officers, reinforced by the entire state constabulary or highway patrol, would not be sufficient to maintain order if violence should erupt (*Allen v. County School Board of Prince Edward City, VA*, 1958).

Hutcheson also ordered a study done on the state of Prince Edward County schools by the school board; the board recruited University of Virginia professor George Zehmer to conduct the study. The NAACP issued a scathing rebuke of the judge's orders to wait ("Letter from Roy Wilkins to the *NY Times*," 1958/1981; "Telegram to *Los Angeles Sentinel* from Roy Wilkins," 1958/1981). Ironically, in his ruling Judge Hutcheson quoted Claude Bowers's *The Tragic*

Era, a Dunning School account of Reconstruction, comparing the Supreme Court's ruling on desegregation to the period of Reconstruction:

> This sad epoch in our history was fomented in no small part, by well-intentioned men in too much of a hurry. The basic lesson wise men have learned from its excesses and its tragedies is that civil rights can be insured and protected only by local government administered by men with a sympathetic understanding of the many facets of the problems involved; men who approach their task in a spirit of friendship and local obligation. Government can succeed only when its mandates deserve and command the respect and the consent of the governed (*Allen v. County School Board of Prince Edward City, VA*, 1958).

Meanwhile, by April 1958, the Prince Edward School Foundation raised enough money to operate a private school system in churches for at least a year if schools integrated. People from across all of the southside counties donated large sums of money to the school foundation, including politicians, business leaders, civic leaders, and church leaders. Governor Almond and company also began formulating legislation that would create tuition vouchers that allowed White parents to use tax dollars to pay tuition to newly created private schools, now known as segregation academies (lists of donors and thank you letters to donors in *Papers of William Munford Tuck*).

At the beginning of 1959, *Allen v. County School Board of Prince Edward County* went on the docket for the US Court of Appeals in the fourth circuit, and the hearing was scheduled for the April term. On May 9, the Court's ruling ordered Prince Edward County to desegregate public schools by September 1, 1959. Later that month, James Kilpatrick gave the commencement address at Farmville High's graduation, and he gave the call to the White community that the time to abandon the public schools was now:

> That the resolute and courageous action of Prince Edward County, taken quietly and unflinchingly after years of patient endurance, and when no other tolerable alternative could be discovered, is in the finest tradition of American political independence. Yours is a small voice, crying boldly to a suddenly and soberly attentive land, that here in Prince Edward, free men survive who face an oligarchy unafraid (Kilpatrick, 1959).

The county heeded his call; on June 26, 1959, the board of supervisors refused to appropriate funds for public schools for the 1959–1960 academic year. This action effectively closed all Prince Edward County public schools after 8 years of court cases and delays.

The shutting down of public schools by Prince Edward County officials was a radical response to *Brown*, one that defies Virginia's reputation as moderate in relation to the Civil Rights Movement. In late August 1959,

Harry Byrd at his annual picnic in Berryville revealed how entrenched the beliefs of White supremacy were in Virginia and that these Virginians were willing to go to extremes to protect this way of life. Stating that the situation "was a tragedy for everyone" and that "the NAACP deliberately and maliciously forced this action upon Prince Edward," Byrd resolved that

> Prince Edward has taken the only action it could take. The county had sought by every honorable means to avoid this step. It was faced with massive integration.... The action that Prince Edward has taken is courageous, and it was thoughtfully and well considered. They remained true to the faith of their fathers (Byrd, 1959).

Byrd concluded his speech by stating the NAACP and the Warren Court's goals were to force mass integration and therefore enforce mass miscegenation (Byrd, 1959). Thus with the same mentality, the White segregationists of Prince Edward County closed the public schools and opened Prince Edward Academy on September 10, 1959.

Prince Edward Academy for the first several years operated out of multiple White churches in Farmville, but several scholars of the time noted that the education was hardly suitable for the White children who attended. The Dean of Longwood College, Dr. Gordon Moss, stated for the press that

> I wouldn't let my son go to it [Prince Edward Academy] for anything in the world. Maybe the kids are doing all right in French and math and English—after all, they have the same teachers they had in the public schools—but they are learning principles that are far from what I would call proper education. How, in a government class, can they teach democracy in such an undemocratic school?" (Goodman, 1981).

In a report for the NAACP on segregation academies, Mary Ellen Goodman (1981) noted that the Whites in the community who disagreed with the segregationists had little recourse to change the school situation:

> And it is extremely difficult or hazardous, psychologically and even socially and economically, for natives to break with or even question native leadership. Breaking with tradition is not a comfortable business at best, and it can become extremely painful when "everybody" who means something to you, "always" has and presumably always will, turns his back—or does worse—the moment your dedication to tradition is observed to waver.

She also noted that the Defenders held a strong grip on the operation of the private school, and their beliefs were certainly influencing the education the students received.

For Prince Edward County's Black community, the closing of schools was a major blow to the morale of the community. For a few months, the local community did their best to place students in schools in neighboring counties, and in November 1959, they formed a group to implement an education program, but it took the state conference of the NAACP time to come up with a plan for educating the Black students and White students who could not afford the private schools. In December 1959, the NAACP made plans to host a Christmas party for all the students who had been shut out of school as a morale boost. Chapters of the NAACP from around the country sent funds, toys, and candy to Prince Edward County for these students. The national office coordinated star entertainment for the children, including commissioning a special album recorded by Mahalia Jackson for them ("Press Release," 1959/1981). This party raised the ire of J. Barrye Wall, as he thought it was the NAACP trying to buy off the Black community to not participate in the private school system a few segregationists had set up for the Black students of Prince Edward County. That same month, Wall and associates established the corporation known as Southside Schools Inc. to form private Black schools, explaining that "we're anxious to provide an education for the Negroes of the county ... the Negroes were making no effort to do it so we decided to go ahead" ("Negro Schools Planned," 1959/1981). Wall wrote in an editorial that week in the *Farmville Herald* that the Christmas party was a "propaganda meeting" for the NAACP and tried in vain to convince the Black community of Prince Edward County to register for the Black schools, but only one student applied ("Negro School Opening Delayed Until September," 1960; Wall, 1959). Meanwhile, the NAACP Legal Defense Fund geared up to challenge the closure of public schools in the county, and the national office in coordination with the Virginia State Conference of the NAACP made emergency plans to bring relief to the students in Prince Edward County.

After the 1954 *Brown* decision, NAACP branches across Virginia prepared to challenge all of the massive resistance efforts across the state, but none compared to the dire situation in Prince Edward County. The national office of the NAACP paid for field workers in Farmville to do community work, focusing on "educating, reeducating, and building self-confidence and reassurance among the parents and children affected that their cause is just and right and must be pursued without faltering." Other NAACP chapters and chapters of Delta Sigma Theta held fundraisers to support this work in addition to providing for educational opportunities outside of the community ("Memo re: Conference of Virginia Schools," 1958/1981). These funds were instrumental in providing educational relief after the schools closed in 1959.

In December 1959, the Virginia State Conference of the NAACP took emergency action to set up a temporary form of education for the students left without schools. The conference placed Prince Edward County under the direction of a local coordinator, Rev. Francis Griffin. Rev. Griffin divided the county into 10 areas, and in each of the 10 areas, the Prince Edward County Christian Association, under the direction of Rev. Griffin, would set up training centers. The state conference gave $16,500 to supervise and educate students for the remainder of the school year. It also paid $8,500 for 61 high schoolers to enroll in Kittrell College, an African Methodist Episcopal college in North Carolina with a high school program. The conference also allotted $1,000 to pay for students enrolled at other schools (Robertson et al., 1981). Reverend Griffin immediately got to work setting up the training centers, which enrolled 650 children (Griffin, 1981; for personal accounts in setting up the training centers and "grassroots schools," see Tillerson-Brown, 2010). These training centers were not intended to be private schools for the children but a temporary relief until the case settled in court. The students at the training centers were under the care of a supervisor and an assistant supervisor at each center. The staff would plan learning programs to engage the students, but each center had students of every grade, so it was difficult to provide the needed differentiation in instruction. However, the centers planned a curriculum that covered health, music, music appreciation, Black history, reading comprehension, English (grammar and writing), arithmetic and applied math, arts, science, social studies, civics, handicrafts, and recreation. With the support of the community, all of the training centers were open by the beginning of April 1960 (Griffin, 1981).

The training centers were meant to be temporary for the 1959–1960 school year. However, when the whole Prince Edward County school board resigned at the end of April, it seemed that these training centers would have to become more permanent (Daugherity & Grogan, 2019, p. xvii). Thus, in June 1960, the NAACP Legal Defense Fund filed another lawsuit on behalf of the Black community in Prince Edward County, *Griffin v. County School Board*. This suit contested the board of supervisors' action to not fund public schools. The board of supervisors' action had tried to make the court orders against the school board to integrate unenforceable. The plaintiffs argued that this was a violation of Virginia's constitution to provide public school and a violation of the due process and equal protection clause in the 14th Amendment. The lawsuit also noted that the board was attempting to lease the public school buildings to Prince Edward Academy, which would be in contradiction to the prior court rulings ("Letter to A. Willis Robertson from J. Segar Gravatt," 1964). Even after the closing of the public schools, Prince Edward County would go back to court.

Conclusion

While the closing of schools demoralized the African American community of Prince Edward County, the spring of 1960 brought some encouraging winds of change, even in southside Virginia. The student sit-in movement swept across the South beginning in February, and in Danville, Virginia, just 90 miles away, Black students sat-in at the local library to protest its segregation. As 1960 rolled on, Rev. A. I. Dunlap, an African Methodist Episcopal minister who had led a church in Prince Edward County and a founding member of the Prince Edward County Christian Association, received assignment to a church in Danville. He would go on to help Danville ministers set up the Danville Christian Progressive Association, a civil rights group that sought to press the city on these issues through direct action. Rev. Dunlap brought his organizing skills from Prince Edward County and helped the Danville group learn as much as they could about building their own movement (Holt, 1965, pp. 20, 61). As 1961–1962 passed, Prince Edward County and Danville activists would lay the foundation and groundwork to set the stage for massive direct-action protests that burst forth in the summer of 1963. It appeared that the White elite had managed to maintain the Virginia way as they countered the initial battles for civil rights in the 1950s and early 1960s, but Black activists across southside persisted, determined to break the grip of White supremacy. As they strategized, so did the White elite, coordinating with their counterparts across the South.

Notes

1. Leidholdt (1997) argued that moderates brought down massive resistance, which in turn brought down the Byrd machine. Lassiter and Lewis (1998) argued that moderates were successful in bringing integration to Virginia due to shifting political representation to more urban areas, a move to more progressive policies in the Democratic Party, and the emergence of a Republican Party unencumbered by the Byrd machine.
2. Kelley (2010) argued in her book on the early 20th-century boycotts in Richmond, Virginia, that progress can be a measure of success, as later movements built on the work of the streetcar boycotts.

References

Allen v. County School Board of Prince Edward City, VA. (1958, August 4). 164 F. Supp. 786 (E.D. Va. 1958) US District Court for the Eastern District of Virginia.

Bonastia, C. (2012). *Southern stalemate: Five years without public education in Prince Edward County, Virginia.* The University of Chicago Press.

Brown v. Board of Education. (1953). School segregation cases—Order of argument record group 267: Records of the Supreme Court National Archives and Records Administration. https://catalog.archives.gov/id/1656509

Byrd, H. (1959, August 29). Excerpts from speech by Senator Harry F. Byrd (D. Va.) at his 37th Annual Orchard Picnic, Berryville, Virginia. In *Papers of Harry F. Byrd*, Small Special Collections. University of Virginia Library.

Byrd, H. F. (1954). Statement by Senator Harry F. Byrd, May 17, 1954. In *Papers of Harry Flood Byrd*, Small Special Collections. University of Virginia.

Crawley, W. B. (1978). *Bill Tuck, a political life in Harry Byrd's Virginia*. University Press of Virginia.

Daugherity, B. J. (2016). *Keep on keeping on: The NAACP and the implementation of Brown v. Board of Education in Virginia*. Carter G. Woodson Institute Series. University of Virginia Press.

Daugherity, B. J., & Grogan, B. (2019). *A little child shall lead them: A documentary account of the struggle for school desegregation in Prince Edward County, Virginia*. University of Virginia Press.

Davis v. County School Board. (1952, March 7). 103 F. Supp. 337 (E.D. Va. 1952), No. 103 F. Supp. 337 (U.S. District Court for the Eastern District of Virginia).

Declaration of constitutional principles. (1956). *Papers of Harry F. Byrd*, Small Special Collections. University of Virginia Library.

Defenders of State Sovereignty and Individual Liberties. (1955). *A plan for Virginia presented to the people of the commonwealth [Pamphlet]*. The Norfolk Public Schools Desegregation Collections, Special Collections and University Archives. Old Dominion University.

Editorial. (1954, May 21). *Farmville Herald*.

Eskridge, S. K. (2021, February 2). J. Lindsay Almond Jr. (1898–1986). In *Encyclopedia Virginia*. Virginia Humanities. https://encyclopediavirginia.org/entries/almond-james-lindsay-jr-1898-1986

Fields, B. J. (1982). Ideology in race in American history. In J. M. Kousser & J. M. McPherson (Eds.), *Region, race, and reconstruction: Essays in honor of C. Vann Woodward*. Oxford University Press.

For state sovereignty and individual liberties: The defenders [Pamphlet]. (1955, August). *Norfolk Public Schools Desegregation collection, MG92*, Special Collections and University Archives, Perry Library. Old Dominion University.

Forgacs, D. (2003). *The Gramsci reader: Selected writings, 1916–1935*. New York University Press.

Geyer, E. (1981). The new Ku Klux Klan. In A. Meier, M. Fox, & R. Boehm (Eds.), *National association for the advancement of colored people*. Papers of the NAACP. University Publications of America. (Original work published 1955).

Goodman, M. E. (1981). Sanctuaries for tradition: Virginia's new private schools. In A. Meier, M. Fox, & R. Boehm (Eds.), *National association for the advancement of colored people*. Papers of the NAACP. University Publications of America.

Griffin, L. F. (1981). Report and overview of Prince Edward County training centers. In A. Meier, M. Fox, & R. Boehm (Eds.), *National association for the advancement of colored people*. Papers of the NAACP. University Publications of America.

Hall, S. (2007). Civil rights activism in 1960s Virginia. *Journal of Black Studies, 38*(2), 251–267.

Henderson, E. B. (1981). Statement on referendum vote. In A. Meier, M. Fox, & R. Boehm (Eds.), *National association for the advancement of colored people*. Papers of the NAACP. University Publications of America.

Holt, L. (1965). *An act of conscience*. Beacon Press.

Kelley, B. L. M. (2010). *Right to ride: Streetcar boycotts and African American citizenship in the era of Plessy v. Ferguson*. University of North Carolina Press.

Kilpatrick, J. J. (1959, May). *Commencement address to Farmville High School.* James J. Kilpatrick Papers, Small Special Collections. University of Virginia.

Kluger, R. (2004). *Simple justice: The history of Brown v. Board of Education and Black America's struggle for equality* (1st Vintage Books ed.). Vintage.

Lassiter, M. D., & Lewis, A. B. (1998). *The moderates' dilemma: Massive resistance to school desegregation in Virginia.* University Press of Virginia.

Lee, B. E. (2015). *A matter of national concern: The Kennedy administration's campaign to restore public education to Prince Edward County, Virginia* [PhD dissertation]. The University of North Carolina at Greensboro.

Lee, B. E., & Daugherity, B. J. (2013). Program of action: The Rev. L. Francis Griffin and the struggle for racial equality in Farmville, 1963. *The Virginia Magazine of History and Biography, 121*(3), 250–287.

Leidholdt, A. (1997). *Standing before the shouting mob: Lenoir Chambers and Virginia's massive resistance to public school integration.* University of Alabama Press.

Letter from Roy Wilkins to the *NY Times.* (1981). In A. Meier, M. Fox, & R. Boehm (Eds.), *National association for the advancement of colored people.* Papers of the NAACP. University Publications of America. (Original work published August 5, 1958).

Letter to A. Willis Robertson from J. Segar Gravatt. (1964, May 8). *Papers of J. Segar Gravatt,* Small Special Collections. University of Virginia.

Lewis, A. (1955, December 30). Segregation group confers in secret: Segregation unit meets secretly. *New York Times.* (1923–Current File).

Memo re: Conference of Virginia schools. (1981). In A. Meier, M. Fox, & R. Boehm (Eds.), *National association for the advancement of colored people.* Papers of the NAACP. University Publications of America. (Original work published June 17, 1958).

Mitchell, H. (1981). A report on the rise of the White citizens councils in the South. In A. Meier, M. Fox, & R. Boehm (Eds.), *National association for the advancement of colored people.* Papers of the NAACP. University Publications of America. (Original work published December 1, 1955).

Muse, B. (1961). *Virginia's massive resistance.* Indiana University Press.

NAACP is prepared to test bid to evade court ruling, Wilkins assures Virginians [Press release]. (1981). In A. Meier, M. Fox, & R. Boehm (Eds.), *National association for the advancement of colored people.* Papers of the NAACP. University Publications of America. (Original work published January 12, 1955).

Negro school opening delayed until September. (1960, January 19). *Farmville Herald. Papers of Harry F. Byrd.* Small Special Collections. University of Virginia Library.

Negro schools planned [*Richmond News-Leader* clipping]. (1981). In A. Meier, M. Fox, & R. Boehm (Eds.), *National association for the advancement of colored people.* Papers of the NAACP. University Publications of America. (Original work published December 15, 1959).

November 26, 1952—school desegregation cases. (1981). In A. Meier, M. Fox, & R. Boehm (Eds.), *National association for the advancement of colored people.* Papers of the NAACP. University Publications of America.

Papers of J. Segar Gravatt, Small Special Collections. University of Virginia.

Papers of James Kilpatrick, Small Special Collections. University of Virginia.

Papers of William Munford Tuck, Special Collections, Swem Library. College of William and Mary.

Press release. (1981). In A. Meier, M. Fox, & R. Boehm (Eds.), *National association for the advancement of colored people.* Papers of the NAACP. University Publications of America. (Original work published December 2, 1959).

Ransby, B. (2003). *Ella Baker and the Black freedom movement: A radical democratic vision.* University of North Carolina Press.

Reid, H. O. (1956). The Supreme Court decision and interposition. *The Journal of Negro Education, 25*(2), 111. https://doi.org/10.2307/2293569

Robertson, R. D., Banks, W. L., & Mason, V. C. (1981). A proposal for temporary and remedial relief for the out-of-school Negro youth of Prince Edward County. Virginia state conference. In A. Meier, M. Fox, & R. Boehm (Eds.), *National association for the advancement of colored people.* Papers of the NAACP. University Publications of America.

Smith Fergeson, L. M. (2001). *Where the south begins: Black politics and civil rights activism in Virginia, 1930–1951* [PhD dissertation]. Emory University. ProQuest Dissertations & Theses Global (304758087). https://www.proquest.com/docview/304758087?accountid=13965

Smith, R. C. (1965). *They closed their schools; Prince Edward County, Virginia, 1951–1964.* University of North Carolina Press.

South Boston rally draws 2,300 crowd: Throng hears Tuck, Denny. (1955). *Reprinted and distributed by the Defenders of State Sovereignty and Individual Liberties.* Norfolk Public Schools Desegregation Collection, MG92, Special Collections and University Archives, Perry Library. Old Dominion University.

Stanley, T. (1981). Statement to the Gray Commission executive committee. In A. Meier, M. Fox, & R Boehm. (Eds.), *National association for the advancement of colored people.* Papers of the NAACP. University Publications of America. (Original work published July 23, 1956).

Statement by Senator Harry F. Byrd on the referendum to be held on January 9, 1956. (1955, December 18). *Papers of Harry F. Byrd.* Small Special Collections. University of Virginia Library.

Statement by Senator Harry Flood Byrd for release in morning papers of Tuesday, November 1, 1955. (1955). *Papers of Harry F. Byrd.* Small Special Collections, University of Virginia Library.

Statement by the Northern Virginia Unit of the Washington Ethical Society. (1981). In A. Meier, M. Fox, & R. Boehm (Eds.), *National association for the advancement of colored people.* Papers of the NAACP. University Publications of America. (Original work published 1956).

Stokes, J., & Wolfe, L. (2007). *Students on strike: Jim Crow, Civil Rights, Brown, and me.* National Geographic Kids.

Sullivan, P. (2009). *Lift every voice: The NAACP and the making of the Civil Rights Movement.* New Press.

Telegram to *Los Angeles Sentinel* from Roy Wilkins, (1981). In A. Meier, M. Fox, & R. Boehm (Eds.), *National association for the advancement of colored people.* Papers of the NAACP. University Publications of America. (Original work published August 6, 1958).

The Gray Amendment and the public school system of Virginia. (1981). Address prepared for telecast over WTAR-TV, January 6, 1956. In A. Meier, M. Fox, & R. Boehm (Eds.), *National association for the advancement of colored people.* Papers of the NAACP. University Publications of America.

Tillerson-Brown, A. (2010). "Grassroots schools" and training centers in the prospect district of Prince Edward County, Virginia, 1959–1964. In T. Hicks & A. Pitre (Eds.), *The educational lockout of African Americans in Prince Edward County, Virginia (1959–1964): Personal accounts and reflections* (pp. 1–18). University Press of America.

Titus, J. O. (2011). *Brown's battleground: Students, segregationists, and the struggle for justice in Prince Edward County, Virginia.* University of North Carolina Press. http://delphi.tcl.sc.edu/library/catalog/offcampus.html?url=https://search.ebscohost.com/login.aspx?direct=true&scope=site&db=nlebk&db=nlabk&AN=365287

Virginia Since May 17, 1954. (1981). In A. Meier, M. Fox, & R. Boehm (Eds.), *National association for the advancement of colored people.* Papers of the NAACP. University Publications of America.

Vrooman, M. (2014, Spring). The doors were locked. In *10 stories, 50 years later.* Longwood University. Small Special Collections, University of Virginia.

Wall, J. B. (1959, December 29). *Let's look at the record [Editorial].* Farmville Herald. Papers of Harry F. Byrd, Small Special Collections, University of Virginia Library.

Wilkinson, J. H. (1968). *Harry Byrd and the changing face of Virginia politics, 1945–1966.* University Press of Virginia.

CHAPTER 3

REMEMBERING THE PAST, LOOKING TOWARD THE FUTURE: THE ROLE OF MEMORY AND RACIAL HEALING IN THE PRESERVATION OF R. R. MOTON HIGH

Dwana Waugh
Sweet Briar College, USA

The 1951 student strike at Moton High School "set in motion events that forever changed the landscape of American education, and arguably marked the start of the modern civil rights movement" (Baker, 2001).

If there was such a thing as a cradle of the Civil Rights Movement, it first rocked here in Prince Edward County (Shanaberger, 1999, p. 1).

Introduction

Fifty years to the day that Black students walked in protest of their segregated high school, Prince Edward County, Virginia, citizens gathered at the same site to celebrate the opening of the Robert Russa (R.R.) Moton Museum. Former students returned to commemorate and celebrate what had become sacred ground to the county and the nation. Flanked with community members, state politicians, and other dignitaries, the importance of this formerly all-Black high school was confirmed. Moton High—once the symbol of educational inequity—had now emerged as a place of racial healing. As former Moton High alum John A. Stokes remarked, "I never thought I'd see the rainbow that I see before me, and the unification of people that I see here" (Woodley, 2001, p. 1). In a sense, Moton represented a microcosm for the nation, a site for public remembrance of a difficult racial past that held promise for a more racially united future. In his keynote speech, National Public Radio host and award-winning author of *Eyes on the Prize* Juan Williams conveyed the dramatic stakes involved with the opening of R.R. Moton Museum. Truth and reconciliation offered the county the chance to find closure for its massive resistance. Williams opined, "We have come to terms with what has happened here and now we can move on. And now we can talk about building coalitions. We can talk about working together" (Woodley, 2001, p. 1).

R.R. Moton Museum represents a growing number of civil rights museums in the United States. It frames Prince Edward County's struggle for school integration as student-initiated civil activism against racial injustice. Contextualized between 1951 and 1964, the museum's six galleries recount the story of student protest involving the *Brown v. Board of Education* case, the disparities of segregated education, the impact of federal court rulings, the indeliberate speed of state policies, the closure of the public schools by the local county, and the reopening of the public school system. All the galleries reveal a bracing, yet uplifting narrative of Black resilience and leadership as the inheritors of American democracy. It was in Prince Edward County, begun with student protest, that the nation moved closer to legal and civil rights. R.R. Moton Museum's mission endeavors "to promote positive discussion of integration and to advance the positions that ensure racial harmony" (Robert Russa Moton Museum, n.d.). The children impacted by inadequate public schools took actions that expanded the concept of constitutional democracy for all Americans. It is here that the museum cites as the "birthplace of the student Civil Rights Movement" (Robert Russa Moton Museum, n.d.).

Established in 2001, Moton Museum began as Prince Edward County's first all-Black high school. It resides in close proximity to one of two local higher education institutions—Longwood University (formerly Longwood College).[1] Between 2011 and 2013, the museum installed its permanent gallery exhibitions, and it was featured on Virginia's Civil Rights in Education Heritage Trail. Deliberately created and maintained, Moton serves as a site of memory that wrestles with a history of stark racial segregation that prevented formal public education for 5 years and a vision of racial harmony that supports equitable education for all schoolchildren. By exploring the antecedents to the preservation of R.R. Moton from school to museum, we can better understand how a community worked to intentionally craft a shared history that encompasses the discomfort from the "hard history" of the past.

Starting in the 1990s, the path to creating Moton Museum was fraught. The contestation over the building symbolized a critical battle over the county's identity and collective memory among its Black and White residents. For the African Americans disproportionately affected by the school closures, they had experienced profound social, economic, and emotional losses. Some Black students attended makeshift, temporary schools or traveled out of the county. Some children and teachers left their families in search of education or employment. A majority of the county's African Americans never experienced formal education due to closed public schools. Most White county residents, from those who remained complacent to the school closings to those who upheld racially segregated schools, came to feel a sense of regret and shame. Other White students directly impacted by the school closings found difficulty in paying the tuition and transportation fees for the alternative segregated private school education. These competing experiences raised powerful feelings. The careful preservation of Moton and the memories it evoked represented an attempt at a communal process that would transform the story of the county's traumatic racist past into one of racial reconciliation and racial healing.

Historian Pierre Nora (1989) argued,

> It is this very push and pull [of history and memory] that produces *lieux de mémoire*—moments of history torn away from the movement of history, then returned; no longer quite life, not yet death, like shells on the shore when the sea of living memory has receded (p. 12).[2]

In other words, sites of memory reveal the tensions between individuals' experience with the past and their reconciliation of it. The retrospectives on *Brown* by the 1980s and 1990s had come to celebrate a racially integrated Prince Edward County as a "model for the nation" and "revitalized" (Phelps, 1994, p. A6; Smith, 1997). Using oral histories and reflections, and newspaper accounts, I trace the intersections of public remembering of massive resistance and argue that saving Moton symbolized an opportunity for the county's Blacks and Whites to reconcile the acrimony of the past. The preservation of R.R. Moton transformed the county from a narrative of racial intransigence to a narrative of racial healing. Moton would stand as a treasured, and important, national landmark.

Beginning of Robert Russa (R.R.) Moton High

In 1939, R.R. Moton High opened as the first public high school for the county's Black schoolchildren. The Martha E. Forrester Council of Women (MEFCW), an all-Black civic organization, had raised enough funds to contribute to its existence. Built to house 180 students, by 1950, the school was bursting at the seams. The student population had grown over 2.5 times its capacity. The local school board constructed three external buildings to serve as temporary space for the overcrowded school. Derisively named the "tar paper shacks" by Moton High students, the shelters were located adjacent to Moton and were covered in tar paper, which resulted in an exceptionally colder and wetter learning environment than the existing school building. Despite the petitions of many Black parents, the school board made little effort to identify more adequate structures for the Black high schoolers.

Moreover, the glaring disparities between Moton High and the all-White Worsham High were equally notable and galling. At Moton, there were no gymnasiums provided, no shower or dressing rooms to accompany physical education or athletics, no cafeteria, no teachers' restrooms, and no school nurse available. While at Worsham High, White students had access to all of those facilities, in addition to an industrial art shop, physics, world history, Latin, advanced typing, wood and metal shop, and drawing classes.[3] To add further insult, for African American students who lived near Worsham, they were unable to obtain free bus transportation to the school. Flossie Hudson recalled having to pay bus fare to attend Moton from her home in Prospect (Hudson, 2012). Moton High School students began to identify the imbalance of access and resources at their school and planned for a direct-action protest: a student strike.[4]

Black Student Activism and *Brown v. Board of Education*

On Monday April 23, 1951, Moton High student leaders decided to stage a walkout in protest to the disparate conditions in the county's segregated schools. Led by Barbara Johns, Carrie Stokes, John A. Stokes, and John Watson, Moton High students piled into the school's auditorium to call for a student strike. Soon thereafter, students marched out of Moton High to the downtown county school board offices. The strike would last nearly two weeks. During this time, Moton students met with the state's chapter of the National Association for the Advancement of Colored People (NAACP) to discuss suing for better material resources.

The NAACP's attorneys had identified a successful equalization campaign throughout the 1930s and 1940s. They brought lawsuits across the US, in federal district courts, to equalize teacher pay disparities between White and Black teachers. The cases resulted in success. The NAACP attorneys intended to create so much financial pressure on local school systems that the maintenance of segregated schooling would be cost-prohibitive.[5]

However, by the late 1940s, the NAACP began to seek out legal cases that would test the constitutionality of school segregation.

For most southern local school boards, officials feared the possibility of racial integration and worked to equalize resources long neglected. In Prince Edward County, local White leaders rushed to build a new all-Black high school, with the same features as the local White high school, on the outskirts of town to address the overcrowding issue. But their actions were too late. When NAACP attorneys Oliver Hill and Spottswood Robinson III agreed to provide legal counsel for Moton High students, if they agreed to demand more than equitable resources, Moton High students consented. They wanted desegregation. Local Black students and parents brought legal suit against the county school board in *Dorothy E. Davis v. The School Board of Prince Edward County*. This case became one of five that formed the landmark Supreme Court *Brown v. Board* case.

White Community Leaders, Massive Resistance, and the Impact of *Brown v. Board of Education* in Prince Edward County

In response to the *Brown* ruling, Prince Edward County's White community leaders resolved to massively resist school integration for 5 years by closing the public schools altogether. They created an all-White segregationist Prince Edward Academy in 1959 for many of the county's White schoolchildren. But most of the county's Black children lost access to any formal education within Prince Edward County. These children would be labeled the "Lost Generation" due to the traumatic disruptions in their education and its subsequent consequences. In 1963, President John F. Kennedy declared that there were only four places in the world where children were denied the right to attend school: North Vietnam, Cambodia, North Korea, and Prince Edward County. As the only democracy on President Kennedy's list, Prince Edward County embodied the hallmarks of an undemocratic state. As a result, the county's massive resistance garnered national and international shame within the free world.

Against the backdrop of the Cold War, Prince Edward County Blacks continued pushing for their civil and constitutional rights within the free world. NAACP attorney Oliver Hill noted that White people are "afraid of the pitiless spotlight of public opinion on Prince Edward [and its school closing]" ("Let's Look at the Record," December 29, 1959, p. 4A). This spotlight drew regional and national press attention to the county and the plight of students ("Catching Up in Prince Edward," 1963; *Christian Science Monitor*, 1962; *Equality Under the Law*, 1966; *The Nation*, 1966; *Saturday Evening Post*, 1961; Smith, 1965; *U.S. News & World Report*, 1963, pp. 44–45).[6]

Along with intensifying student civil rights protests across the US, Prince Edward County students picketed for desegregated public accommodations. They also pursued legal action to challenge the closed public schools. Local minister Rev. L. Francis Griffin, known as the "Fighting Preacher," signed onto another NAACP court case to question the constitutionality of Prince Edward County's massive resistance effort. In 1964, the Supreme Court heard *Griffin v. School Board of Prince Edward County* and ruled that African American schoolchildren's equal protection under the law was violated. The county's public school system was ordered to reopen by the fall of 1964.

Once the schools reopened, Prince Edward County residents contended with the aftermath of its massive resistance. Prince Edward County Public Schools (PECPS) needed to rebuild its infrastructure: faculty, resources, and student body. In the fall of 1964, 1,500 African American students returned to the public school system. Fewer than 0.5% of the county's White schoolchildren returned. Throughout the 1970s and 1980s, the public schools strove to create desegregated education, which required the infusion of White students. Whites regretted the negative media coverage of the school closing era. Gretchen Rogers argued that "sometimes it feels like reporters are locking us into what happened in the 1959–1964 period and I hate that" (Smith, 1997, p. 11). Many Blacks struggled with anger and insecurities. They wondered why Whites hated them so much to keep them from an education (Groff, 2016, pp. 23–24).[7]

Black Community Activism for the Legacy of Robert Russa Moton School

African American civic and social organizations also worked to shape the legacy of the school closing era. Black organizations—such as the MEFCW, the Branch-Moton Historical Society, and the Branch-Moton Alumni Association—gave voice to saving the school building. These organizations were forged in or by racial segregation. They diligently worked to increase access and improve material conditions for Prince Edward County's local Blacks. Members of these groups recounted their unique experiences within segregation and the impact massive resistance had on them. As a result, these memories cultivated perceptions of race relations in the county. They gave shape to the locus of Black memory of segregated education and massive resistance.

Formed in 1920, the MEFCW began as a group focused on the racial uplift of their community. They focused on improving educational opportunities for Black children. Throughout the 1920s and 1930s, the MEFCW collected and raised funds to support the expansion of higher grades in Prince Edward County. They worked to enhance the educational opportunities and resources of the county's Black children. Some members tutored children who were locked out of the public school system during the school-closing era.

The Branch-Moton Historical Society was named for the all-Black elementary and secondary schools in the county. Headed by local attorney James Ghee, the society focused on the memory of Black resistance and activism. In the 1980s, they raised funds and applied for a historical marker signifying the importance of R.R. Moton High with the state's Department of Conservation and Historic Resources. The marker, erected outside of the Moton building, symbolized the importance of Black history in the county.

The Branch-Moton Alumni Association formed in September 1976 to connect members of the Lost Generation ("Branch Moton Alumni Plan Annual Meeting," 1980, p. 8A; "Branch, Moton Grades Form Alumni Group," 1976, p. 1; "Griffin Monument Ceremony Monday," 1988, pp. 1–2). Approximately 400 alumni converged on Prince Edward County from near and far locations to reconnect with each other, reflect on the school closing period, and work actively to improve the PECPS system. The alumni group formed committees to identify potential funding sources, provide scholarships to local public-school students, and improve library resources. To honor the county's "Fighting Preacher," Rev. L. Francis Griffin, they initiated an annual scholarship (1976) and raised funds to erect a monument (1988) in his name ("Griffin Monument Ceremony Monday," 1988, pp. 1–2).[8]

During the debates over what to do with the former R.R. Moton High School building in the 1990s, African Americans capitalized on the importance of situating the African American experience into the history of both the county and the nation.[9] Indeed, local Black preservationists attested that granting federal national historic site status to Moton would legitimate Prince Edward County's Black residents' school desegregation experiences. As Vera Allen argued, saving Moton was "the last battle for our legacy" (Baker, 2001).[10] While most Whites viewed the effort to preserve Moton as invoking the racial strife and bitterness of the school-closing era, many African Americans had a different relationship with the space. Most Blacks, however, attended Moton. They taught there. They staged a protest movement there. And they had built a community at Moton. As a result, Black organizations, such as the MEFCW, fought to obtain ownership over the school. MEFCW president Vera Allen, a former Black teacher displaced during the school closings, and Branch-Moton Historical Society president James Ghee, a former Black student in eighth grade when the schools closed, latched onto the idea of converting the old Moton High School into a national historic site and civil rights museum. For Allen and Ghee, Moton symbolized the quintessential American story of grit, hard work, and persistence in the face of all odds. Commemorating Moton would redeem the county for its period of school closing and tie it with other struggles for civil rights. Moton's national status helped to reconcile Whites and Blacks in a town where tensions went unspoken and hurts unhealed.

The attempts to determine the usability of the Moton building and its historical significance seemed promising. In 1990, the Virginia Department of Historic Resources (DHR) deemed the R.R. Moton building to be "historically significant" (Applin, 1990, pp. 1, 4).[11] Two years later, various community groups were invested in the purposing or repurposing of Moton. PECPS, Longwood College, and the MEFCW agreed that they would share the usage of the five-acre plot of land on which R.R. Moton resided. Longwood was experiencing an increase in student enrollment, and they sought out athletic fields for the larger number of student athletes ("Longwood, PE Schools Ponder Shared Land Deal," pp. 1, 10).

Community Tensions in Remembering R.R. Moton School

However, the memories of the county's racially stratified past confronted the present battles over spacing. By the early 1990s, PECPS and Longwood College were outgrowing their facilities. Farmville Elementary, housed at the Moton building, served the county's fifth graders. As they outnumbered the space, the county board of supervisors began construction on an addition to Prince Edward County Elementary School, located near the local middle and high schools. The new addition cost $1.5 million dollars and was planned for completion by the fall of 1996. PECPS superintendent James M. Anderson admitted that the school system was "strapped for finances." Although the building and land on which Moton sat represented a valuable location, he ensured that the school board did not plan to abandon the Moton building structure ("Longwood, PE Schools Ponder Shared Land Deal," p. 10).

By the early 1990s, the college experienced dramatic growth in its undergraduate student population. To accommodate growing needs, Longwood scouted the county for more land. Because the Moton site was adjacent to the college, as Superintendent James Anderson implied, it was prime real estate. In fact, Longwood had a history of purchasing land surrounding the college, which was part of the predominately Black neighborhoods along Griffin Boulevard. School officials' assurances that Moton would remain untouched, and Longwood's expanding landscape, did little to quell the concern among members of the African American community.

Blacks recalled the erasure of their presence and history in the county's history. Charles Herndon (1992) recalled how his aunt lost her home for the purpose of building Longwood's basketball courts. The college declared her land eminent domain and paid her one-fourth of its real value, while Whites who lived on valuable land close to the college could maintain their homes "because they are landmarks" (p. 57).¹² As one former Moton student argued,

> I think [Blacks are] looked at basically as people who can be disposed of and manipulated. One of the things I was trying to talk to some of our Black leaders about is the displacement of some Black people on Griffin Boulevard for Longwood College. That to me seems like Longwood officials are saying we don't have to worry about Blacks. We can do what we want. We won't even take the time to try to look for an effective way or a secondary campus (Foster & Foster, 1993, p. 34).

MEFCW president Vera Allen (1992) argued that if Moton became "a national monument, [state and county leaders] can't take it. The school board can't take it from us. And we're afraid they might." This fear of loss is no surprise, as the county and state had once successfully eliminated public education for Black children.

The board of supervisors, responsible for funding the public school system, "made it equally clear that they do not intend to let the historical society's plans interfere, slow down or impede their decision regarding disposition of the property" ("Prince Edward County Can Make History," 1993, p. 1B). Just days before the DHR set to confer Moton's landmark status, the county board of supervisors drafted a letter to the Virginia DHR requesting a deferral of Moton's landmark status. County administrator Mildred Hampton feared the landmark designation would interfere with their efforts to sell the property and the land.

The DHR had worked for nearly three years with the MEFCW to identify the historical significance of R.R. Moton School. With the objection of the board of supervisors, the process seemed delayed indefinitely (Joachim, 1995a, p. 12). According to Julie Vosmik with the Virginia DHR, the county leadership had "let us know that as long as they are the owners, they don't want" the historic designation to be granted to Moton (Joachim, 1995a). She admitted it surprised her because she thought there was a lot of local support. For the county supervisors, selling Moton would offset the $1.1 million the county spent on building a new wing for the county's fifth graders (Joachim, 1995b, pp. 1, 3; see also Joachim, 1995a, pp. 1, 12). As board of supervisors chair Hugh E. Carwile Jr. stated, "Selling Moton would limit what Longwood could do.... That's valuable land out there and someone might have a use for it" (Joachim, 1995a, p. 12).

Over 200 people packed into First Baptist Church the week after the board of supervisors and county public school system withdrew support for Moton's historic designation. James Ghee of the Branch-Moton Historical Society asked attendees whether Moton should be preserved "and used as some sort of tribute to the segregation struggle," and he was met with astounding support (Joachim, 1995b, pp. 1, 3; Ruff, 1995a). As former

Moton High parent Fred Reid argued, Moton was a place of national importance. "People at R.R. Moton School sacrificed themselves for this country. That's why we should preserve it, so it will go down in history. So people will know the sacrifices that were made in Prince Edward County" (Joachim, 1995b, p. 3). By the meeting's end, $1,000 was raised to preserve R.R. Moton.

During the summer of 1995, a compromise had been reached. The county would sell R.R. Moton to the MEFCW for $300,000 and its surrounding lands to Longwood College for $700,000 (Joachim, 1995c, pp. 1, 12; Joachim, 1995d, pp. 1, 8). The MEFCW would pay $200,000 over a 2-year period by December 31, 1997. The other $100,000 would be financed by the Prince Edward County board of supervisors with a 6% loan. Toward the end of 1995, the purchase, and hence historic designation, of R.R. Moton seemed almost assured.

But Longwood administration halted their end of the deal. Since they would be paying more for the land than the MEFCW would pay for the building, college officials insisted that the $700,000 was too expensive. Longwood vice president Richard V. Hurley agreed to pay a little over half of what the county requested but felt the price had been inflated.[13] Board of supervisors administrator Mildred Hampton countered that the county had assessed the land's value in 1993 and determined that the land was worth the price requested. For the county board of supervisors, the omission of Longwood from this tandem property deal would not be sufficient. The fate of Moton's preservation rested on simple economics. The county leadership claimed Longwood's withdrawal from the deal was an issue of financial stability. Without funds to offset the cost of the new fifth-grade school addition, Moton needed to be sold to the highest bidder.

Some local Blacks believed a more insidious rationale explained the precarious future status of R.R. Moton. Former African American county schoolteacher Thomas Mayfield asserted that White county leaders wanted to demolish the school. Longwood's reservation in purchasing the land was merely an excuse. Mayfield argued that Moton represented "an eyesore and a mindsore. It's a reminder of the stupidity of those who perpetuated the closing of the schools and segregation" (Baskervill, 1996, pp. 4–5). Board of Supervisors chair Hugh Carwile seemed to confirm Mayfield's suspicions. He told a visiting *Washington Post* reporter that perhaps "the county may be better served if the building is removed" because "it's like a constant reminder, like rubbing salt in a wound" (Baker, 1993, p. B3).

By the fall of 1995, the future of Moton remained uncertain until a groundswell of support came from the local press, perhaps from one of the most unexpected places: The *Farmville Herald* began to support the efforts of Black community members in preserving the school. The newspaper had once given voice to the county's most segregationist actions. Run by steadfast segregationist J. Barrye Wall Sr., the *Farmville Herald* endorsed massive resistance and the private all-White Prince Edward Academy. However, by the mid-1990s, the paper had notably shifted its perspective. According to editor Ken Woodley, conferring a historic designation on R.R. Moton *and* selling it to the MEFCW was a positive, win-win solution. A museum "would be a positive way to preserve both the building and the community's role in the historic Supreme Court decision." Woodley contended that, like other sites of Virginia's Civil War history, Moton was a "rare piece of American history ... [whose] preservation should be pursued" ("Prince Edward Can Make History," 1993, p. 1B).

City Boosterism and the Case for R.R. Moton's Preservation

City boosters identified a sellable feature of the preservation of Moton: heritage tourism. Virginia's rich legacy in colonial, Revolutionary War, and Civil War histories abound across the state. In Prince Edward County, these histories often intersect. By the late 20th and early 21st centuries, the focus on civil rights memory and history attracted more attention from city boosters. Heritage tourism composed a large portion of Virginia businesses, yielding approximately 3.6 million Black visitors out of 33 million a year (Ruff, 2004). The former state secretary of commerce and trade, Michael J. Schewel, explained that "African American tourists to Virginia spend more and stay longer than the average visitor" (Orth, 2004, p. A1). Marketing Moton as "ground zero" for the Civil Rights Movement, where student protesters marched to change segregated schools, held high promise for the rural town. For a community with a low median income, attracting visitors made sense for its economy.[14] In the South, heritage tourism is the "second fastest growing market segment of tourism" (Walker, 2005, p. B2).[15] Lacy Ward Jr., field representative for Democratic representative Lewis F. Payne, argued, "For us to not realize the unique stature in which this building stands, and to not capitalize on that for its economic and historical value, would be a mistake" (Joachim, 1995d, p. 8).

Black community leaders shared the story of Moton as a means to market and fundraise for saving Moton. The MEFCW's advertisement in *Historic Preservation* in early 1996 outlined the significance of saving R.R. Moton in a six-page feature article. As a result, letters poured in from over 23 states with financial contributions in tow. Lacy Ward Jr. argued that this outpouring of support from beyond the county illustrated the broad marketability of making Moton into a museum. Here, Ward argued, local residents protested civil injustices and defied massive resistance to emerge "as a model of rural school system" (Ward, 1996, p. 2B). Ward served as a member of Governor George Allen's Regional Economic Development Advisory Council, which serves the Farmville region. Likening the Moton story to that of outside interest in Civil War tourism, Ward argued that Farmville had a proximate location, is accessible, and continued the Virginian tradition of heritage tourism from colonial, Revolutionary War, and Civil War histories to civil rights.

The actions taken by the local press, city boosters, and African American activists resulted in a shared vision of racial healing through the preservation of Moton. Ken Woodley saw city boosterism with a greater opportunity to reshape Prince Edward County's public image. Like Vera Allen, Woodley asked his readers to understand the historic importance of preserving R.R. Moton:

> Let's put this in perspective.... Dozens of Civil War battle sites are state and national parks. There are hundreds of acres set aside to commemorate the Civil War in the Farmville area along. Dedicating less than one acre to the other—but no less significant—"Civil War" fought for civil rights is certainly not asking too much.... We can't rewrite history. But we can make it (Smith, 1997, p. 3).

In a similar vein, Hampden-Sydney College president General Samuel Vaughan Wilson offered a community space on campus to wrestle with the "cruel injustices perpetuated in the past by Caucasian Americans upon African Americans, as well as upon Native Americans.... We must face up to this sad period and learn from it" (Woodley, 2003, p. 2A). While largely silent during the school-closing era, Hampden-Sydney sought not to take credit for a more integrated public school system but to reflect on the county's race relations. Wilson emphasized the importance of reconciling the harsh realities of racial prejudice with the democratic promise of constitutional freedom.

Moments of Reconciliation: Hampden-Sydney College's Symposium—"Prince Edward Stories: Race, Schools, and America"

In October 1999, Hampden-Sydney College held a symposium titled "Prince Edward Stories: Race, Schools, and America." Held over 4 days, the "symposium sought a retrospective on the 40th anniversary of civil rights in education." Hampden-Sydney president General Samuel V. Wilson underscored that

> ... the closing of the schools ricocheted and echoed around the world.... We peg it to the 40th anniversary. We don't celebrate it. We mark it and then stop and think about it. It is not something to celebrate (Woodley, 1999a, pp. 1–2).

It was free and open to the public. The symposium provided a means to reconcile the memories of massive resistance. For Whites, it was not that massive resistance did not happen. It did. But the era of educational trauma needed healing. For Blacks, the symposium provided African Americans with a space to be seen and heard. The losses they faced could be recast as the essence of American democracy and equality before the law (Woodley, 1999a, p. 2).

In one especially poignant moment at the symposium, Dr. Ray A. Moore Jr. and Willie Shepperson embraced each other at a panel discussion. Moore was the vice chairman of PECPS from 1959 to 1969. Shepperson, a Moton alum, was considered a firebrand. The last time they saw each other was at a contentious 1969 school board meeting, where Shepperson accused Moore of failing to assist Black schoolchildren and advocated for a growing sense of Black power (Sauder, 1969, p. 7).

This embrace was surprising in that Dr. Ray A. Moore Jr. had warned President Wilson from holding the symposium. To Moore, it would create more problems than it solved. After seeing Shepperson's name listed on the planned program, Moore warned President Wilson that "you have at least one person on your program that I guarantee that his ugly rhetoric will cause fist fights to break out in the audience and they'll be bloody noses" (Woodley, 1999b, pp. 1, 10, 12).

In his panel, titled "Children's Stories: Being First, Being Left Out, Wondering What's Going On," Shepperson illuminated the trauma Black children faced during the school-closing era.

> If you'll notice, most of the children in Prince Edward County, Black and White, when they start telling these stories, the tears come, the pain is real. Why? Because nobody took the time during our era to bring in the counselors to teach you how to deal with this (Woodley, 1999b, p. 10).

Both men's memories differed in reflecting on the school closings. To Moore, a public retelling of the pain and devastation caused by massive resistance only served to unearth racial tensions and animosities. To Shepperson, a collective remembering of the closed public schools highlighted how invisible and ignored county Blacks had felt by the existing power structure.

However, Willie Shepperson demonstrated magnanimity in universalizing the memory of school closings to all county residents. He argued that White students suffered the same as Blacks did

> We can criticize and eulogize. We can do all these things that give us some sort of emotional release, and that is good. We need that, but we also need to lay a basic foundation for today's young people so they can learn from our mistakes and move forward (Woodley, 1999b, p. 10).

Making the memory of school closings a shared experience, Black and White citizens could find closure. African Americans could voice the hurt and pain that they experienced 40 years prior, and Whites could reconcile their shame.

Blacks' capacity for forgiveness was rooted in a Christian tradition. Rev. Everett Berryman believed Prince Edward County was chosen by God "because of the strength of the families and faith in this community" (Scoggin, 2016, p. 7). Mickie Carrington admitted that she retained anger and hatred toward Whites. She learned to release her emotions after hearing a sermon about "letting go of what happened to us and that God had a purpose for allowing it to happen" (Moton Museum & Longwood University, 2014, pp. 28–29). Both Berryman and Carrington represented part of the populations locked out of the public schools. Yet, rather than focusing on the realities of the school closures as victims, they articulate a strength and persistence through adversity.

In a meaningful way, Shepperson and Moore symbolized what the preservation of R.R. Moton meant to the county. When Shepperson called Moore for an embrace, he also stated that the best mechanism for healing in Prince Edward County was the preservation of R.R. Moton. Its transformation into a museum

> ... is an opportunity for this community to work together and show that we can work together as a community of mankind and let this be a symbol of what we must never do again. We can do this together.... It can be a part of the process of healing. We can never make it go away but we can make it heal (Woodley, 1999b, p. 10).

Charlotte Womack expressed the pain of missing out on public education, but she insisted that the goal of remembering the school closings was to "not try to make somebody else feel like they still have to pay for those four years," which met resounding applause from the audience (Woodley, 1999b, p. 10). Sam Putney, a White Prince Edward Academy graduate, was angry with his parents' generation for closing the schools. Yet he admitted his astonishment in the level of forgiveness African Americans expressed (Woodley, 1999b, p. 10).

The mechanism for healing in the county, Shepperson argued, was R.R. Moton. Its transformation into a museum

> ... is an opportunity for this community to work together and show that we can work together as a community of mankind and let this be a symbol of what we must never do again. We can do this together.... It can be a part of the process of healing. We can never make it go away, but we can make it heal (Woodley, 1999b, p. 10).

Moore expressed his "conversion" to this collective remembrance. Devoid of expressed anger, the racial harmony in Prince Edward County would depend on African Americans' capacity to forgive.

Conclusion

The impact of Black activism, the local press, marketing strategy, and the community-wide symposium effectively secured the support of county residents, along with that of the nation. In 1996, the MEFCW established the charter status for the R. R. Moton Museum. By 1998, the National Park Service granted National Historic Landmark status to Moton. By 2001, the museum opened to the public with great fanfare. Not only had R.R. Moton been saved from destruction, but it also represented a community effort to produce a counternarrative of racial healing to offset the narrative of racial bigotry.

Since the museum's opening in 2001, Moton has held community gatherings for county residents, scholars, and guests to reflect on the 1959–1964 Prince Edward County era. Each Monday, museum staff hold a brown bag lunch series, along with other physical and virtual events. Visitors are encouraged to participate in open dialogs and discussions about local history and its national importance. In Mickie Carrington's case, Moton provides a salve for the community: "Each time I attend something, like the Brown Bag Lunches on Mondays, [it] helps me heal more and more. Someone else's story helps me heal so the [Moton] Museum has really been my healing ground" (Moton Museum & Longwood University, 2014, p. 29).

In many ways, Juan Williams's call for building coalitions at the opening of the R.R. Moton Museum had been symbolized by the preservation of Moton. The preservation process embodied both the collaboration between the county's White and Black residents and the coming to terms with the harsh reality of the school-closing period. Virginia is home to many historical sites that stand as a monument of historical importance: George Washington's Mount Vernon, Thomas Jefferson's Monticello, and James Madison's Montpelier express the vitality of early US leadership. Many monuments have been erected to honor the memory of the cataclysmic battle between the Union and the Confederacy during the Civil War. The Appomattox Court House, a national historic park, has insisted that it shows the "beginning of peace and reunion."[16] It is fitting that in Virginia—a state marked by the weight of national history—Moton too represents an important and valuable location that highlights tragedy but also the reconciled memories of its peoples.

Historian W. Fitzhugh Brundage's (2008) *Southern Past: A Clash of Race and Memory* asserted that historical memory is the result of intentional creation. Much of the history of the South has given precedence to the memory of White southerners, often at the peril of Blacks. Brundage provided a glimmer of hope that while "Black history may not crowd the southern landscape to the extent that White history does … it is present and visible to a degree that was unimaginable as recently as two decades ago" (p. 315). In Prince Edward County, African Americans gave shape to the design of the memory of massive resistance in preserving R.R. Moton. The narratives of Black resilience and Blacks as upholders of constitutional principles in the 1950s and 1960s emerged in the presentation of R.R. Moton's history.

As a site of memory, Moton reveals an uplifting community narrative of racial progress. Prince Edward County had shifted from its segregationist intransigence, which resulted in 5 years of closed public schools, to racially integrated spaces that provide hope for future opportunities. The community's motivation to unite around the site of Moton—whether for economic, psychological, racial, or deeply personal reasons—demonstrates the community's attempts to refashion a new legacy. Moton, once a site of racial injustice and educational inequity, resurfaced as a site of reconciliation. This newer understanding of massive resistance made Moton a "museum and monument to the Lost Generation" ("Moton's Impact in the Community and Beyond," 2014).

Progress, it seems, defined other aspects of the county's society. By the late 1960s, African Americans had obtained positions of power in Prince Edward County's political and educational structures. Blacks gained a stronger role in county and electoral politics. In 1979, LaVerne Pervall and James Massey were appointed to the Prince Edward County school board. James Ghee, in the same year, was elected to the county board of supervisors as the first African American to serve. In 1984, Carl Eggleston was elected to the town council.

In the decades after the school closings, Prince Edward County's public schools had begun to reflect a desegregated institution. The racial composition of classes matched that of the county. The teaching staff and county principals generally reflected the numbers of the county's Black-to-White ratios. By 1999, PECPS superintendent Margaret Blackmon noted that 90% of the county's children attended public schools. This demonstrated an increase in racial integration within the school system.

However, while there was measurable progress in the county, there were growing divisions between Black and White students in the public schools. In the 1980s and 1990s, public school students often found themselves attending racially homogenous classes. The county school board had instituted policies that increasingly, and disproportionately, tracked African American students into remedial and average classes. White students had disproportionately been tracked into talented and gifted classrooms. The local NAACP advocated for more equitable procedures in assigning students to classes. Moreover, in 1994, the school board cut the budget of students receiving free and reduced lunches, impacting many Black and low-income students (Prince Edward County Public School Board Minutes, 1986, 1994a, 1994b).

In her influential essay, "The Long Civil Rights Movement," historian Jacquelyn D. Hall (2005) averred that limiting the master narrative of the Civil Rights Movement to what scholars call the "classic phase" of the movement from 1954 to 1968 produces a narrative that "simultaneously elevates and diminishes the movement" by freezing our collective memory to a "triumphal moment in a larger American progress narrative" (p. 1234) The framing for Moton centers the narrative on student protest and their successful universal push for equality under the law. Saving Moton resulted in a curated narrative of triumph. While Brundage encouraged us to understand the intentional process of *how* historical memories are made, Hall (2005) cautioned us to interrogate *why* we remember the past so that we can speak more "effectively to the challenges of our time" (p. 1234).

Notes

1. Prince Edward County, Virginia, is home to two colleges and universities: Hampden-Sydney College (1775) and Longwood University (1839). Hampden-Sydney is an all-male private liberal arts college. Longwood—once known as Longwood College—was formerly an all-female state teacher-training school. Today it is a coeducational publicly funded state university.
2. For scholarship on the historical memory and public commemorations, see Brundage (2008), Foote (2003), Klugh (2005), Landsberg (2004), and Sturken (1997). For discussions of civil rights memory, see Dwyer and Alderman (2008) and Romano and Raiford (2006).
3. The gross inequities between the White and Black high schools in Prince Edward County are addressed in *Davis v. Prince Edward County*.
4. For more on the 1951 Moton High student strike, see Kluger (1976), Smith (1965), and Stokes and Wolfe (2008).
5. For some Virginia-based NAACP equalization cases, see *Margaret Smith. v. School Board of King George, Virginia and T. Benton Gayle, Division Superintendent* (1946), *Arthur Freeman, et al. v. County School Board of the Chesterfield County et al.* (1948), and *Alice Lorraine Ashley v. School Board of Gloucester County, Virginia and J. Walter Kenny, Division Superintendent* (1948).
6. For other award-winning media coverage of massive resistance, see Murrow (1959).
7. For oral histories of anger regarding massive resistance, see Eanes (1998), Carrington (2012), and Brown (2012).
8. The monument stood five feet tall, composed of granite and bronze. It sat at the intersection of South Main Street and Griffin Boulevard in Farmville, Virginia. The monument cost $2,235, but the alumni group raised $3,407.
9. The names and reuse of the former R.R. Moton High building had changed since the schools reopened in 1964. In the late 1960s, Moton was renamed the Mary E. Branch Elementary School, No. 2. By the late 1970s, the building's name had changed to Farmville Elementary School. By the early 1990s, the public school system utilized the building for the county's fifth-grade students.
10. For more about R.R. Moton's historic designation process, see Applin (1990, p. 1), "Longwood, PE School Ponder Shared Land Deal" (1992, pp. 1, 10), Baskervill (1996, p. 5), and Ruff (1995b, p. B4).

11. The Virgina DHR noted R.R. Moton's eligibility. The school was erected with Works Progress Administration funds. Prior to 1939, there was no Black high school in the county. Blacks had to go to Mecklenburg County or the Thyne Institute to complete their education.
12. For more on Longwood's expansion into historically Black communities' land, see Baker (1993, p. B3) and Ruff (1995c, p. C8).
13. Hurley stated Longwood had acquired a contracted survey of the land's assessment, which totaled $375,000. This price, he argued, the college would pay. See Joachim (1995e, pp. 1, 3).
14. Prince Edward County's median income in 2000 was $31,301 (http://www.co.prince-edward.va.us/demographics.html). The national median income in 2000 was $41,990 (http://www.census.gov/compendia/statab/files/income.html).
15. For further scholarship on heritage tourism, see Smith (1982) and Eskew (2001). See also Brundage (2008).
16. This is quoted on the Appomattox Court House, National Historical Park, Virginia website: https://www.nps.gov/apco/index.htm

References

Allen, V. (1992, August 21). *Interview with Ken and Laurie Hoen for Farmville, Virginia, not our children*. Virginia Historical Society. Mss15 N8437a.

Applin, J. (1990, September 15). PE school may become a landmark. *Farmville Herald*, 1.

Baker, D. (1993, March 6). Support for a Virginia school and its history lesson. *Washington Post*, B3.

Baker, D. (2001, March 4). Closed. *Washington Post Magazine*. https://www.washingtonpost.com/archive/lifestyle/magazine/2001/03/04/closed/327020e7-afb0-43ec-9c43-2b6bcbbc7b57

Baskervill, B. (1996, March 21). Battle to save historic Farmville school. *Richmond Free Press*, 4–5.

Branch Moton alumni plan annual meeting. (1980, August 29). *Farmville Herald*, p. 8A.

Branch, Moton grades form alumni group. (1976, September 10). *Farmville Herald*, p. 1.

Brown, W. (2012, May 5). Interview with Robert Sawyers. What's Your Story?, for Learn, Preserve, and Empower, Desegregation of Virginia Education (DOVE), Farmville, Virginia.

Brundage, W. F. (2008). *Southern past: A clash of race and memory*. Harvard University Press.

Carrington, A. P. (2012, May 5). Interview with Ann Jimerson. What's Your Story?, for Learn, Preserve, and Empower, Desegregation of Virginia Education (DOVE), Farmville, Virginia.

Catching up in Prince Edward. (1963, August 9). *Time Magazine*.

Christian Science Monitor. (1962, April 5). Microfilm.

Dwyer, O. J., & Alderman, D. H. (2008). *Civil rights memorials and the geography of memory.* Center for American Places at Columbia College Chicago.

Eanes, S. (1998, April 15). Interview with Veronica Myers and Loretta Parham. Civil Rights in Prince Edward County. Longwood University.

Equality under the law: The lost generation of Prince Edward County [Film]. (1966). Encyclopedia Britannica Educational Corp.

Eskew, G. T. (2001). From Civil War to civil rights: Selling Alabama as heritage tourism. *International Journal of Hospitality Administration, 2,* 201–214.

Foote, K. (2003). *Shadowed ground: American landscapes of violence and tragedy.* University of Texas Press.

Foster, V. W., & Foster, G. A. (1993). *Silent trumpets of justice: Integration's failure in Prince Edward County.* U.B. & U.S. Communications Systems, Inc.

Griffin monument ceremony Monday. (1988, September 2). *Farmville Herald,* pp. 1–2.

Groff, J. (2016, Spring). Just drive. *Their Voices, Our History: Stories of Prince Edward County, Virginia, 2*(2), 23–24.

Hall, J. D. (2005, March). The long Civil Rights Movement and the political uses of the past. *Journal of American History, 91*(4), 1234.

Herndon, C. (1992, August 20). Interview with Ken and Laurie Hoen for Farmville, Virginia, not our children. Virginia Historical Society. Mss15 N8437a.

Hudson, F. S. (2012, May 5). Interviewed with Robert Sawyers. What's Your Story?, for the Learn, Preserve, and Empower, Desegregation of Virginia Education (DOVE) Project, Farmville, Virginia.

Joachim, M. B. (1995a, February 15). Landmark bid stalled for Moton school. *Farmville Herald,* p. 12.

Joachim, M. B. (1995b, February 22). Citizens show support for Moton school. *Farmville Herald,* pp. 1–3.

Joachim, M. B. (1995c, July 14). PE supes reveal Moton plan. *Farmville Herald,* pp. 1–12.

Joachim, M. B. (1995d, July 14). Public speaks on Moton sale plan. *Farmville Herald,* pp. 1–8.

Joachim, M. B. (1995e, October 13). Longwood, PE supervisors face off over land deal. *Farmville Herald,* pp. 1–3.

Kluger, R. (1976). *Simple justice: The history of Brown v. Board of Education and Black America's struggle for equality.* Vintage Books.

Klugh, E. L. (2005, Summer). Reclaiming segregation-era, African American schoolhouses: Building on symbols of past cooperation. *Journal of Negro Education, 74*(3), 246–259.

Landsberg, A. (2004). *Prosthetic memory: The transformation of American remembrance in the age of mass culture.* Columbia University Press.

Longwood, PE school ponder shared land deal. (1992, April 3). *Farmville Herald,* pp. 1, 10.

Moton Museum and Longwood University. (2014). *10 stories 50 years later.* Prince Edward Stories, pp. 28–29.

Murrow, E. R. (1959). *The lost class of '59: A study of Virginia's massive resistance: Segregation and the Norfolk Public Schools.* City of Norfolk. https://dove.gmu.edu/index.php/2018/09/05/the-lost-class-of-59-a-study-of-virginias-massive-resistance-segregation-and-the-norfolk-public-schools/

The Nation. (1966, November 14). Microfilm.
Nora, P. (1989, Spring). Between memory and history: Les Lieux de Mémoire. *Representations,* (26), 12.
Orth, K. (2004, May 15). Warner: Students will be helped. *Richmond Times-Dispatch,* (p. A1).
Phelps, T. (1994, May 17). A model for the nation: Virginia county has high-quality, integrated schools. *Newsday,* p. A6.
Prince Edward can make history by preserving the Moton-Branch school [Editorial]. (1993, November). *Farmville Herald,* p. 1B.
Prince Edward County Public School Board Minutes. (1994a, June 22).
Prince Edward County Public School Board Minutes. (1986, May 7).
Prince Edward County Public School Board Minutes. (1994b, August 3).
Robert Russa Moton Museum. (n.d.). http://motonmuseum.com
Romano, R. C., & Raiford, L. (Eds.). (2006). *The Civil Rights Movement in American memory.* University of Georgia Press.
Ruff, J. C. (1995a, February 2). Saving Moton school is hope: Effort underway in Prince Edward. *Richmond Times Dispatch.*
Ruff, J. C. (1995b, June 26). Farmville Elementary was a site of historic struggle. *Richmond Times Dispatch,* p. B4.
Ruff, J. C. (1995c, December 3). Longwood seeks help to get land. *Richmond Times Dispatch,* p. C8.
Ruff, J. C. (2004, May 15). Warner: Students will be helped. *Richmond Times Dispatch.*
The Saturday Evening Post. (1961, April 29). Microfilm.
Sauder, B. (1969, May 1). Prince Edward: Pride's 2 sides. *Richmond News Leader,* p. 7.
Scoggin, M. (2016, Spring). No fear, just faith. *Their Voices, Our History: Stories of Prince Edward County, Virginia,* 2(2), 7.
Shanaberger, F. (1999, October 29). Prince Edward stories: Race, schools, America— Smith: A civil cradle. *Farmville Herald,* p. 1.
Smith, R. C. (1965). *They closed their schools: Prince Edward County, Virginia, 1951–1964.* University of North Carolina Press.
Smith, S. A. (1982). The old South myth as a contemporary southern commodity. *Journal of Popular Culture, 16,* 25–26.
Smith, R. C. (1997, Winter). Prince Edward County: Revisited and revitalized. *Virginia Quarterly, 73*(1), 1–27.
Stokes, J., & Wolfe, L. (2008). *Students on strike: Growing up African American in the segregated South (with H. Viola).* National Geographic.
Sturken, M. (1997). *Tangled memories: The Vietnam War, the AIDS epidemic and the politics of remembering.* University of California Press.
U.S. News & World Report. (1963, September 30). pp. 44–45. Microfilm.
Walker, D. (2005, June 30, B2). Civil rights museums: A tourism magnet in many cities. *Richmond Free Press.*
Wall, J. B. (1959, December 29). Let's look at the record. [Editorial]. *Farmville Herald,* p. 4A.
Ward, L. Jr. (1996, March 29). Civil rights museum would boost economy. [Editorial]. *Farmville Herald,* p. 2B.
Woodley, K. (1999a, September 8). Prince Edward stories: Rewards outweigh the risks. *Farmville Herald,* pp. 1–2.

Woodley, K. (1999b, November 3). ....You are my brother. *Farmville Herald*, pp. 1, 10, 12.
Woodley, K. (2001, April 25). The rainbow I see before me. *Farmville Herald*, p. 1.
Woodley, K. (2003, April 30). Moton museum honors Wilson. *Farmville Herald*, p. 2A.

Additional Reading

Patterson, C. (Dir.). (2014). *Moton's impact in the community and beyond* [Virtual community panel]. R.R. Moton Museum.

CHAPTER 4

THE POWER OF THE PRIMARY SOURCE: USING A CASE STUDY OF PRINCE EDWARD COUNTY, VIRGINIA (1951–1964) TO TEACH THE CIVIL RIGHTS MOVEMENT

Caitlin B. Maloney
Southern New Hampshire University, USA

Introduction

In 2010, the National Assessment of Educational Progress found that only 2% of high school seniors could accurately answer questions about *Brown v. Board of Education* (cited in Southern Poverty Law Center, 2024). This statistic is troubling and points to a serious issue in the way secondary educators approach the topics of *Brown v. Board* and the Civil Rights Movement. The prevailing pedagogy surrounding instruction on the Civil Rights Movement stems from the "master narrative" (Jeffries, 2019), where well-known figures—such as Martin Luther King Jr., Rosa Parks, and Thurgood Marshall—dominate instructional time. While these activists are undoubtedly important figures of the Civil Rights Movement, the master narrative neglects the actions of ordinary people and grassroots movements that served as the backbone of the Civil Rights Movement. The prevailing pedagogy has oversimplified and shortened the struggle of African Americans in our nation; it ignores the scope of the Civil Rights Movement at the local level.

What can be done to improve student engagement, increase understanding of historical topics, and actively combat the master narrative? In my previously published thesis, "A Microhistory of Prince Edward County, Virginia, 1951–1964: Civil Rights Curriculum for Virginia's Secondary Educators," I answered these questions. I created a curriculum aligned to Virginia Department of Education Standards of Learning for US history and world history 1500–present and learning objectives for African American history. This curriculum served as a free resource for educators to help them approach the Civil Rights Movement in a more meaningful and engaging manner through the use of primary sources focused on how young adults and teenagers experienced and influenced the Civil Rights Movement.

Prince Edward County

Prince Edward County (PEC), Virginia's, history from 1951 to 1964 fully encapsulates the various narratives of the Civil Rights Movement ranging from grassroots organization to young adult/student activism, *Brown v. Board*, *Brown* II, the National Association for the Advancement of Colored People (NAACP), massive resistance, the Student Nonviolent Coordination Committee, and the Southern Christian Leadership Conference. Martin Luther King Jr. spoke in PEC. Robert F. Kennedy visited and spoke about PEC. The county's history represents the Civil Rights Movement at the microlevel.

Studying PEC places the contributions of ordinary people from the rural south at the forefront while simultaneously addressing the "Long Civil Rights Movement." Years of struggle, oppression, activism, and case-building preceded *Brown v. Board*, and years of segregation followed *Brown v. Board*. With case studies like the one present in "A Microhistory of Prince Edward County," students experience the full scope of this monumental legislation from its inception to its fulfillment. The county also offers a glimpse of the Civil Rights Movement from the perspective of school-aged individuals. High schoolers, not adults, created PEC's legacy.

The students of Robert Russa Moton High School, led by 16-year-old Barbara Johns, walked out of their high school in 1951 to protest unequal conditions in the county's racially segregated high schools. These same students called Oliver Hill and asked that the NAACP represent their cause, which was initially declined, until a group of Moton students voted to protest for integration rather than additional funding to improve Moton High

School. The students of PEC played an integral role in the *Brown v. Board* case, comprising nearly 75% of the plaintiffs. And, unfortunately, all school-aged children in the county experienced the collapse of the public school system due to massive resistance in 1959. Learning about the students who fought for justice and equality and the students who bore the brunt of massive resistance recenters conversations about the impact that young people have in our country. As educators, our job is to equip students for their future. Part of molding well-equipped students is empowering them to know that a better future is possible and that they are capable of being instruments of change; lessons of the past that students can relate to are the key to that empowerment.

One of the biggest questions going into the creation of "A Microhistory of Prince Edward County" stemmed from my own ignorance on the topic. I grew up in neighboring Charlotte County, Virginia. I went to Fuqua School, from kindergarten through second grade, which evolved from Prince Edward Academy, an all-White private school that opened during PEC's public school closures. I played sports, went to the best movie theater within a 50-mile radius, and dined in PEC (and still do). Why did I not know more about the county's history during the civil rights era? Because I did not know much about the history, I failed to teach my high school students an in-depth history of the county. I wanted to do better for my students but had to figure out why I, as a historian from southside Virginia, lacked the knowledge and resources to teach about the history of my region.

Jill Ogline Titus addressed the issue of the lack of academic publications about PEC's role in the Civil Rights Movement in her 2011 publication, *Brown's Battleground: Students, Segregationists, and the Struggle for Justice in Prince Edward County, Virginia.* Titus introduced the concept of the Virginia Way, where the genteel politics of Virginia created a semblance of peaceful relations between White and Black citizens so long as Black citizens accepted the status quo of Jim Crow (Titus, 2011, p. 275). The Virginia Way represented a "polite" White supremacy in which

> white leaders demanded that blacks approach them as supplicants grateful for the patronage of their "betters." So long as blacks remained in their place, leaders strategically shunned the crassness of segregation by ordinance. They insisted that tradition, example, and social pressure could successfully guard racial lines (Titus, 2011, p. 287).

The Virginia Way focused on appearance; race relations seemed commendable in Virginia when compared to the overt racial violence found in the Deep South. The Virginia Way strategically and purposefully tried to ensure there were no spectacles for the media or the federal government to pinpoint so that segregation and White supremacy could continue as normal within the state.

Christopher Bonastia (2012) echoed Titus's analysis in *Southern Stalemate: Five Years Without Public Education in Prince Edward County, Virginia*. Like Titus, Bonastia pointed to the lack of overt violence between White and Black PEC residents as a cause for less media and federal attention. Both authors credit the political environment of Virginia, but Bonastia expanded by adding that "black Prince Edwardians pursued justice primarily via legal mobilization" (pp. 8–9). He argued that if Prince Edwardians had employed more direct-action campaigns in their quest for justice, they would have been met with violence and, in turn, garnered increased media and government attention (p. 8).

Segregationists is PEC did not blow up churches; they did not spray protestors with firehoses or beat nonviolent protestors in the streets. They made calculated arguments of the lost cause genre, pointing to states' rights, federal overreach, and conservative fiscal policy to systematically dismantle public education in the county. An overlooked headline compared to murder, public beatings, and acts of domestic terrorism. Both Titus and Bonastia arrived at the conclusion that PEC lacks academic attention today because it lacked media and government attention during the civil rights era due to there being very little instances of overt violence coupled with a more palatable version of oppression. Because the media and government dialed in on locations in the Deep South experiencing intensely violent events, the struggle in PEC remained a more localized issue during the events and after. As someone who has lived in southside Virginia for the past 22 years, I find the argument of Titus and Bonastia to be fair, especially coming from individuals who are not from southside.

In addition to their arguments, PEC's history has remained a niche topic of interest for scholars who stumble on its history because it is not something Prince Edwardians or Virginians in surrounding counties want to be associated with (Daugherity & Grogan, 2019, loc. 4848). It is hard to face the reality that one's close ancestors may have played a part in the school closures. It is also hard to face the reality that one's community members were deprived of an education and to know that the effects of education deprivation have had lasting impacts in one's community. For those who lived through the school closings, there may be shame or embarrassment attached to their being denied an education. To admit that one's family lacked the economic resources to send children to an all-White private school goes against the pride associated with being blue collar. Jeffrey Travers's and Stanley Milgram's (1969) 6 degrees of separation rule shrinks in rural communities.

Once I figured out why I had not been taught a comprehensive history of PEC, I began to question how we should teach about PEC and the Civil Rights Movement as a whole. Hasan Kwame Jeffries's (2019) *Understanding and Teaching the Civil Rights Movement* addressed the dominance of the master narrative in civil rights curriculum (pp. 5–6). The master narrative does not provide a comprehensive study of the Civil Rights Movement because it perpetuates the narrative of prominent figures, institutions, and legislation starting with *Brown v. Board* and ending with the assassination of Martin Luther King Jr. This creates a shortened timeline of the fight for equality, freedom, and justice African Americans have undertaken since the first enslaved Africans arrived at Jamestown in 1619. Only bolstering prominent figures, institutions, and legislation ignores that fact that the Civil Rights Movement was a people's movement, and it is impossible to accurately teach about a people's movement if we do not approach the topic through the lens of people's history.

The master narrative also poses issues with student engagement. Year after year after year, students learn the prevailing narrative of the Civil Rights Movement with the same characters and events. Adam Sanchez (2019), in "Rosa Did More Than Sit and Martin Did More Than Dream," stated, "Because most students learn about the civil rights movement long before they enter high school, many come to my class with the idea that they have already learned all there is to know about it" (p. 41). Unsurprisingly, learning about the same thing with little to no additional context for years is boring and therefore leads to low levels of student engagement. Sanchez implored educators,

> As teachers, we also have to move beyond teaching the movement focusing solely on prominent leaders. If it had not been for ordinary people, we might not even know the names of people like Martin Luther King Jr. or Malcolm X (p. 42).

The master narrative also focuses on the nonviolent direct-action campaigns of the Deep South and juxtaposes it to the Black Power Movement of the northern states, which furthers the inaccurate depiction of racism, segregation, and oppression as being a strictly southern issue. The violence that plagued campaigns in the Deep South caused border states like Virginia to be overlooked. The fear of "extremist" views from the Black Power Movement in the North caused border states like Virginia to be overlooked. The only issue with completely abandoning the master narrative is that students need to know prominent figures, institutions, and legislation of the Civil Right Movement; rather than completely throwing away the master narrative, educators need to enrich its narrative. Let the master narrative serve as background knowledge, and use studies, like the one present in "A Microhistory of Prince Edward County" to fill in the gaps.

Primary Source Analysis

At the forefront of my curriculum was an attempt to encourage student engagement via primary source analysis presented through various types of individual and group activities. David Kobrin (1995) outlined the importance of primary source analysis in secondary classrooms in "Let the Future Write the Past: Classroom Collaboration, Primary Sources, and the Making of High School Historians." Kobrin went against the traditional Socratic seminar style of instruction. He stated, "Our job as teachers, then was more to help kids discover for themselves the power inherent in the historian's methods of work than to dominate the stage with our presence" (p. 508). While Kobrin's findings came with no empirical data to prove that primary-source-based instruction leads to improved student outcomes, Dr. Avishag Reisman (2011) put the theory of document-based learning to the test.

In his study, Reisman (2011) found that students who participated in document-based learning via the Reading Like a Historian curriculum scored higher on multiple-choice questions from standardized tests than students in control classrooms where instructors "placed greater emphasis on memorization and factual recall" (p. 41). Kobrin and Reisman both provided lived examples of the power of the primary source in the high school classroom and concluded that the best way for students to learn history is for students to *do* history. These findings also fall in line with how instructors from other subject areas approach teaching their students. Math teachers model skills, and then students actively participate by solving equations. English teachers model reading and writing skills, and then students read and write. Science teachers model the scientific method, and then students become scientists during labs. History teachers have to allow the space for our students to practice being historians.

After deciding that primary sources would form the basis of the curriculum, I began my quest to learn more about the topic. There is a significant amount of research conducted on PEC as it pertains to the student walkout at Robert Russa Moton High School in 1951; *Davis v. Prince Edward*; *Brown v. Board*; the public schools closing in 1959; the various ways children received an education while schools were closed; and the schools reopening and integrating after the *Griffin v. Prince Edward* decision of 1964. *A Little Child Shall Lead Them: A Documentary Account of the Struggle for School Desegregation in Prince Edward County, Virginia* by Brian J. Daugherity and Brian Grogan (2019) provided a prologue that detailed the history of PEC's African American community during the Reconstruction Era. Grogan and Daugherity then carved out seven distinct chapters that chronologically addressed PEC from 1951 to 1966 followed by an epilogue that addressed more modern sentiments surrounding the school's closing by those who either planned the closures or were affected by them.

A Little Child Shall Lead Them proved to be one of the most useful resources available for learning what I had not been taught about PEC and informing the direction of the curriculum I created. Each primary source was accompanied by an overview by Daugherity and Grogan that explained the document's context and importance and a set of open-ended but helpfully guiding discussion questions. This collection of primary sources embodied the idea of the Long Civil Rights Movement by providing the breadth of the struggle for equality in PEC. It also highlighted the importance of allowing the reader to decide for themselves how to interpret the history of PEC via primary source analysis; it makes the task of doing history less exhausting and intimidating by having a variety of primary sources available in one place. By having these primary sources in a single collection, Daugherity and Grogan (2019) increased accessibility to PEC's history for the public, who may not have the knowledge, resources, and/or perseverance to do the research themselves.

As a formerly overworked and tired teacher, I knew the curriculum I created needed to be all-encompassing with lesson plans, vocabulary lists, lesson overviews, teacher directions, student directions, primary sources, questions, activities, discussion prompts, and writing prompts. The difference in a subject being taught in-depth and being brushed over often depends on the availability of resources. Time was the most valuable resource I had as a teacher, and there was never enough of it, especially during my first year in the classroom. Anything that can lighten the workloads for teachers and give them time back is a valuable classroom resource. In an era where 44% of male and 57% of female K-12 teachers experience feeling burned out in 2022 (Marken & Agrawal, n.d.), and "a staggering 55% of educators" thought about leaving the profession in the same year (Walker, n.d.), discussing the best pedagogy is not enough. Scholars have to stop telling teachers about the best ways to teach and leaving them to figure out how to implement pedagogy on their own. Scholars have to do a better job of, at the very least, providing examples of their pedagogical theories in action and, at the most ideal, creating free or highly affordable curriculum aligned to the pedagogical theories they espouse.

Grogan and Daugherity (2019) and the Robert Russa Moton Museum's (n.d.) physical displays and virtual museum tour inspired the manner in which primary sources were organized and presented in my curriculum. Like *A Little Child Shall Lead Them* ... , the Moton Museum also journeyed farther into the past when telling the history of PEC, going all the way back to the Declaration of Independence and Bill of Rights to remind visitors of the promises made in our founding documents (Robert Russa Moton Museum, n.d.). This reminder is important because it contextualizes the rights of the people and responsibilities of the government to the people in contrast with the reality of what many Americans experienced; it also displays the Long Civil Rights Movement.

Lessons in the Curriculum

"Lesson 1: Reconstruction Amendments, *Plessy v. Ferguson*, and Jim Crow Review" (Maloney, 2022, pp. 70–72) borrows from Grogan and Daugherity (2019), as the Reconstruction Era was chosen as the curriculum's starting point. Students are first tasked with defining the Reconstruction Era and listing the presidents during the era by practicing active recall and relying on their prior knowledge. Next, students use the internet to read the 13th, 14th, and 15th Amendments to the US Constitution and then have to summarize their meaning in their own words. After defining the Reconstruction amendments, students learn about the origins of Jim Crow laws via a podcast. With the knowledge of how Jim Crow laws evolved, students then use a historical marker to learn about Homer Plessy and the *Plessy v. Ferguson* case. Each section of the lesson was designed for students to use their prior knowledge and provided sources to answer questions in writing (read and respond). To close the lesson is a discussion on Jim Crow laws that is to be facilitated by the instructor. The class is to come up with a list of at least 10 Jim Crow laws (e.g., segregated public restrooms, movie theaters, bans on interracial marriages, etc.). After the class has compiled their list, students compare their list to one from the internet (source provided). They then discuss the following as a class:

> What laws did we not think of in our list? What laws surprised or shocked us? What laws had we not heard of before? Are there any laws we do not understand, and how do we find a way to understand them better? (Maloney, 2022, p. 72).

This lesson is primarily for review but also serves as an "equalizer" for students who may not have much or strong prior knowledge of the Reconstruction Era going into the curriculum.

"Lesson 2: Jim Crow Laws in Prince Edward County, Virginia" (Maloney, 2022, p. 72) feeds off of the closing discussion in Lesson 1, where students identified and discussed Jim Crow laws. In "Lesson 2" students match primary source material that explains the lived experience of Jim Crow laws in PEC, Virginia, and match them to the primary source quotes coinciding with Virginia Jim Crow legislation. Selected quotes from Twitty J. Styles's *Son of Prince Edward County*, Alfred L. Cobbs's *Locked Out: Finding Freedom and Education after Prince Edward County Closed Its Schools*, Dorothy L. Holcomb's *Educated in Spite of ... A Promise Kept*, and interviews of Ernestine Herndon and Betty Ward Berryman comprise "Column A" in this lesson's matching activity. "Column B" pulled selected quotes from the Virginia Constitutional Convention of 1902, the Virginia General Assembly's "1926 Supplement to the Virginia Code of 1924; Containing All the General Laws of 1926 with Full Annotations," Thomas Johnson Michie's *The Code of Virginia as Amended to Adjournment of General Assembly 1930*, and the "Virginia Health Bulletin: The New Virginia Law to Preserve Racial Integrity" from the Document Bank of Virginia. The lived experiences of people being compared to legislation holds power; when students are able to understand how laws affected ordinary people, Jim Crow laws seem less abstract and distant.

"Lesson 3: Fighting Against Public School Segregation in Prince Edward County, Virginia" (Maloney, 2022, pp. 75–109) contains three separate activities. Each activity addresses different learning styles to create differentiation and to allow students whose strengths may fall outside of read-and-respond learning activities to shine. Lessons 1 and 2 do not employ much collaboration between students, as their main goal is to serve a quick review so students can explore Lessons 3–7 with a better understanding of why the Civil Rights Movement happened and the atmosphere of PEC prior to the 1951 student walkout.

In Lesson 3, "Activity 1: Barbara Johns and the 1951 Student Walkout Newspaper Article" is a group activity where students are challenged to create a newspaper article, with the resources at their disposal, that summarizes the causes and effects of the 1951 student walkout at Moton High School. Students are provided with selected quotes from four primary sources: Barbara Johns's unpublished memoir transcript held by the Robert Russa Moton Museum, "Interview with John A. Stokes" from the "Voices of Freedom" collection at Virginia Commonwealth University Libraries, "Interview with Oliver W. Hill Sr." from the "Voices of Freedom" collection at Virginia Commonwealth University Libraries, and "Students' Attorneys File Petition to End Segregation in Schools: R.R. Moton Pupils End 2-Week Strike" from *The Farmville Herald and Farm-Leader*. This activity is collaborative, requires primary source analysis, involves hands-on learning skills and creativity, and requires the use of direct quotes from primary sources as evidence to student summarization of events. Teachers could incorporate further learning styles by requiring students to present their articles to the class.

Lesson 3's "Activity 2: Role Play of NAACP Lawyers Building the *Davis. V. Prince Edward* Case" is another small-group activity where students analyze photographs submitted as evidence of unequal conditions between all-White schools and all-Black schools in PEC. Students use photographs of Farmville High School (all White), Worsham High School (all White), and Moton High School (all Black) to find examples of equal conditions and unequal conditions and write them into a T-chart. They then use a copy of the US Constitution to create a written argument that answers the following questions:

> Were the conditions at black and white public high schools in Prince Edward County, Virginia equal or unequal? Use evidence from the photographs and Constitution to make a compelling argument as if you were a lawyer arguing this case before the Supreme Court (Maloney, 2022, p. 94).

Students then present their written arguments as oral arguments to the class; teachers are given the option to have students vote for the best oral argument or to facilitate a discussion about the various strengths of each group's arguments to close the lesson. This activity not only challenges students to think like historians but also asks them to think, case build, and argue like lawyers while incorporating primary source analysis, evidence-based writing, and oral presentation in a collaborative setting.

The last activity in Lesson 3, "Activity 3: Reading and Annotating the Original Opinion filed in *Dorothy E. Davis et al. versus County School Board of Prince Edward County*, Virginia, Civil Action No. 1333," rounds out Activity 2 by allowing students to see the conclusion of the evidence they previously analyzed. In this activity, students, at the direction of the teacher, will practice annotating documents to find the relevant people, places, and information in the Virginia Supreme Court decision of *Dorothy E. Davis et al. versus County School Board of Prince Edward County*. The class reads through the document out loud, together, and students say "stop" when they believe important people, places, and/or information are revealed in the text. Once the class has discussed whether the information is relevant, they will underline or highlight the information and take any notes, then move on through the text. Once the annotation portion of this activity is completed, students work in pairs to come up with a short summary of the *Davis v. Prince Edward* case, which includes the following information: "Where was the case tried (what court)? When was the case tried? Who was involved in the case (judges, lawyers, plaintiffs, defendants, etc.)? What did the court decide in the case?" (Maloney, 2022, p. 95).

"Lesson 4: Massive Resistance" (Maloney, 2022, pp. 110–117) contains one activity, titled "Activity 1: Massive Resistance at the Federal, State, and Local Levels." The entire activity is a read/analyze-and-respond style and outlines the responses to the *Brown v. Board* decision at separate governmental levels (federal, state, and local). The lesson begins with a review of the 1954 *Brown v. Board of Education* Supreme Court decision, and I supply supplemental information that accompanies direct quotes from the decision. After reviewing *Brown v. Board*, students are introduced to *Brown* II, which again, is an overview written by me with direct quotes from *Brown* II included. Moving from *Brown* II, students learn about the Southern Manifesto on Integration and are provided with excerpts from the document to answer analysis questions that require evidence from the text to support answers. The next primary source comes from Virginia governor J. Lindsay Almond's school integration speech of 1959. Following Almond's speech is a Defenders of State Sovereignty and Individual Liberties recruitment pamphlet from Old Dominion University's Perry Library. The last primary source in this activity is a *Farmville Herald* article titled "Public Hearing on School-Less Budget June 23." From these sets of primary sources, students will understand how resistance to *Brown v. Board* operated on the federal, state, and local levels.

"Lesson 5: The Lost Generation 1959–1964" (Maloney, 2022, pp. 118–147) is comprised of three activities. "Activity 1: Gallery Walk and Analysis Tic-Tac-Toe" (Maloney, 2022, pp. 118–129) requires peer collaboration, movement around the classroom, and student choice. This activity also includes the perspectives of Black and White Prince Edwardians during the public school closures.

A study by Dr. Edward H. Peeples conducted in 2002 for the Virginia General Assembly estimated the actual number of black students affected by the five years of closed public school at nearly 2,700... . Estimates from field surveys conducted by the American Friends Service Committee (AFSC) in 1964 indicated that several hundred poor white children were also affected by the crisis (Daugherity & Grogan, 2019, pp. 209–212).

While a vast majority of the students effected were Black, it is important for students to understand the effects of PEC closing its public schools on the entire community, which includes providing information about White students who were shut out as well as White students who had the opportunity to attend Prince Edward Academy. Students also need to hear from Black students who received forms of formal and informal education while locked out of the county's public schools.

In "Activity 1: Gallery Walk and Analysis Tic-Tac-Toe," teachers post excerpts from the following primary sources around the room at five stations: Dorothy L. Holcomb's *Educated in Spite of ... A Promise Kept* (Station 1); Alfred L. Cobbs's *Locked Out: Finding Freedom and Education After Prince Edward County Closed Its Schools* (Station 2); interviews of John Noel (Station 3), Darlene Ferguson Bratcher (Station 3), and Shirl Nunnally Early (Station 4) from the Robert Russa Moton Museum's "Student Voices" collection; a *TIME Magazine* article titled "Integration: Dickie's Decision" (Station 5); and an interview of Richard Moss by Casey Bainbridge from *Longwood University Students—Moton Museum, Joint Venture, All Eyes on Prince Edward County* (Station 5). When these primary sources have been posted at different locations around the room, they become stations for students to analyze each primary source individually within a set timeframe determined by the teacher (e.g., 5 minutes per station). This gives students the opportunity to get out of their desks and to move around the classroom, which serves as an attention span reset. At the same time, they are collaborating with peers in their small groups to analyze the primary sources and answer questions from the "Primary Source Analysis Tic-Tac-Toe" chart. This chart contains a total of nine questions presented in a three-by-three chart. Students answer three questions in a row—horizontally, vertically, or diagonally—with a total of eight possible question combinations at each station. Table 4.1 provides a visual of the activity's questions and question combinations. Each student in the small group must answer a different set of question combinations at each station to encourage collaboration over copying. While encouraging peer collaboration, this activity also champions student choice by allowing students to pick the questions they want to answer/analyze about each

Table 4.1

Primary Source Analysis Tic-Tac-Toe

1. Did they receive a formal education during the school closings?	2. What did they go through to receive an education? If they did not receive an education, what did they do instead?	3. Did any organization/people help them during the school closings? If so, list the organizations/people that helped and explain how they helped.
4. If you could ask them two questions about the school closings, what would those questions be?	5. Free space: Write down the quote from this station that resonates with you the most or means the most to you.	6. How did they initially react to the school closings and how did their reaction to the school closings change or remain the same over time?
7. Did they ever leave Prince Edward County during the school closings? If so, where did they go and why? If not, why did they stay and why?	8. Did they graduate high school? What did they do after graduating?	9. Did they attend the Prince Edward County Free Schools? Explain why or why not.

Source: Developed by Caitlin Maloney.
Question combinations: 1, 2, and 3; 1, 5, and 9; 1, 4, and 7; 2, 5, and 8; 3, 5, and 7; 3, 6, and 9; 4, 5, and 6; 7, 8, and 9.

source. The activity closes with a class discussion about how many of the individuals in the primary sources went on to become educators and why that may have been a career path these people chose.

"Activity 2: Was the Lost Generation Truly Lost?" (Maloney, 2022, pp. 130–146) introduces students to various organizations and political figures who stepped in during the county's public school closures to provide formal and informal means of education from 1959 to 1964. Students analyze and answer questions from the following primary sources: "American Friends Service Committee Prince Edward County Emergency Project," William J. vanden Heuvel's *Hope and History: A Memoir of Tumultuous Times*, Neil V. Sullivan's *Bound for Freedom: An Educator's Adventures in Prince Edward County, Virginia*, Robert F. Kennedy's speech at Kentucky's Centennial of the Emancipation Proclamation in 1962, "Interview with Dr. Milton A. Reid, Voices of Freedom: Videotaped Oral Histories of Leaders of the Civil Rights Movement in Virginia," the Southern Christian Leaderships Conference's "Report of the Director: Semi-Annual Report, November 1–April 20, 1960," an interview of Betty Berryman by Autumn Uptain titled "An Interesting Time" in *Longwood University Students—Moton Museum, Joint Venture, 10 Stories 50 Years Later*, a photograph titled "Crowd and Police Near First Baptist Church, Farmville, Va., August 1963" from Virginia Commonwealth University Libraries, a photograph titled

"Martin Luther King Jr. Visiting Students in Prince Edward County, VA, When Schools were Closed" from Virginia Union University, and "Prince Edward County, Virginia Desegregation, Including Federal Court Order to Reopened Schools," from the Library of Congress's NAACP papers. After answering the read-and-respond analysis questions, student will participate in Activity 3.

"Activity 3: Four Corners Class Vote and Debate" (Maloney, 2022, p. 147) reinforces student choice and is another opportunity for students to get up from their seats, move around the room, and collaborate with peers. Teachers either print out or write *American Friends Service Committee* (paper 1), *the John F. Kennedy Administration* (paper 2), *Southern Christian Leadership Conference and the Student Nonviolent Coordination Committee* (paper 3), and *the NAACP* (paper 4) on four separate sheets of paper. These pieces of paper are then posted in the classroom's four corners. Students are instructed to think about the organization that they found to be the most beneficial for PEC. Once students have had adequate time to form their opinion, they travel to the corner of the room that coincides with their choice. When all students have gotten to their corners, they work with others at their station to create an evidence-based argument that displays why their choice of an organization conducted the most beneficial work in PEC. After students have prepared their arguments, they will present to the class, and the class will have a friendly debate about their arguments. Students then have the opportunity to change their decision on the most important organization involved in PEC if they were swayed by another group's argument.

"Lesson 6: Desegregation at Long Last—1964" (Maloney, 2022, pp. 148–158) contains three activities and is the final lesson in the curriculum. "Activity 1: Analysis of the 1964 *Griffin V. Prince Edward Ruling*" (Maloney, 2022, p. 148) is an individual read-and-respond analysis of excerpts from *Griffin v. County School Board of Prince Edward County* and is followed with a classroom discussion answering the following prompt: "How did the *Griffin v. Prince Edward* decision affect Prince Edward County, and how would it affect public education in the United States? What was its impact?" (Maloney, 2022, p. 148). This activity brings the history of PEC during the Civil Rights Movement to a natural end for students.

"Activity 2: Effects of the School Closings on Prince Edward County Children" (Maloney, 2022, pp. 150–156) is a small-group analysis activity where students collaborate with peers to analyze findings from Robert L. Green's and Louis J. Hofmann's "A Case Study of the Effects of Educational Deprivation on Southern Rural Negro Children." This activity requires that students understand how to read graphs with an x-axis and y-axis. As a precaution to not assume that all students in the class are proficient in this skillset, I included a labeled example of how to read and discern information from these types of graphs, which is depicted in Figure 4.1. Students and teachers will analyze this graph together to ensure students understand how to move forward during the rest of the activity.

Figure 4.1

Regression of Grade Equivalent Score on Age for the Stanford Achievement Paragraph Meaning Subtest

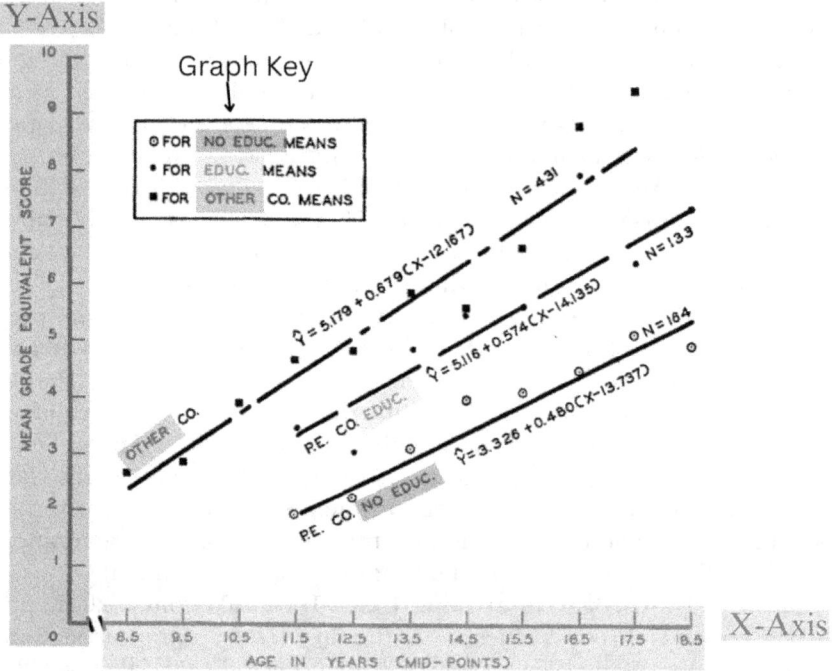

Source: Adapted from Green and Hofmann (1965).

After practicing analyzing graphs as a class, students work in small groups to analyze results from the Stanford Achievement Test on paragraph meaning, word meaning, language, spelling, arithmetic reasoning, and arithmetic comprehension, and results from the Stanford-Binet IQ Test. Each graph contains results for three separate groups tested in the study: no education (Prince Edwardian African American children who received no formal education during the school closures), education (Prince Edwardian African American children who received a formal education during the school closings), and other county (African American children from neighboring counties who did not experience a disrupted education from 1959 to 1963). After analyzing the study results and answering analysis questions, students are tasked with answering the following writing prompt: "Based on your findings in the analysis questions, did the school closings have a positive or negative impact on children in Prince Edward County, Virginia?

How would the learning loss experienced by students effect the rest of their lives?" (Maloney, 2022, p. 156). While the first activity in this lesson brings students to a natural conclusion of the events that transpired in PEC from 1951 to 1964, this activity focuses on the effects of those events. It shows students the impact of history on the average person and goes beyond simply detailing people living through events.

"Activity 3: Project Graduation Cap" (Maloney, 2022, pp. 157–158) represents the culmination of the information students have gathered throughout the entire curriculum through a creative expression outlet. Teachers are provided with a graduation cap template that students are to decorate individually. The purpose of the cap is either to honor a particular student from PEC from the curriculum or to honor all of the students of the county who were denied an education during the school closings. While not an extremely intellectual activity, students get the chance to reflect on their learning throughout the curriculum and to choose how they would like the history of PEC to be remembered and viewed by others who see their artwork. This assignment was heavily inspired by the Butterfly Project from the Holocaust Museum Houston (n.d.).

Conclusion

Much research—consisting of primary, secondary, and tertiary sources—went into the creation of "A Microhistory of Prince Edward County" in terms of both finding analysis items for students and ensuring the curriculum was created with evidence-based pedagogy in mind. While the curriculum was originally designed to be taught as a complete unit, each activity or lesson could also serve as a stand-alone assignment without students feeling lost or confused. It is completely understandable that some teachers and classrooms may not be able to commit the recommended 2 weeks of instructional time to cover the entire curriculum, so the pacing needs of individual teachers and classrooms were considered in the curriculum's framework.

Though not mentioned in "A Microhistory of Prince Edward County," another point to strengthen student engagement with the history of PEC is the shared experience of learning loss between post-COVID-19 students and the "lockout" students of PEC. During the COVID-19 pandemic, 95% of countries closed schools "for a median of 17 weeks," which led to learning loss and increases in dropout rates worldwide (Moscoviz & Evans, 2022, pp. 1–2). Our students today do not have to imagine being sent home from school and not returning for an extended period of time. They do not have to imagine navigating education outside of a physical school building. They do not have to imagine their homes turning into classrooms; they do not have to imagine their parents, relatives, or guardians serving as interim teachers; they do not have to imagine how it felt to be a student with no graduation ceremony, or prom, or sports/clubs; they do not have to imagine being separated from their friends and favorite educators. And, most importantly, they do not have to imagine the uncertainty of living through turbulent times and facing them with resiliency. These statements are not meant to downplay what took place in PEC from 1959 to 1964, but ignoring the parallels would be ignoring an opportunity for current students to directly relate to the experiences of PEC's lockout generation.

I wish I could say that I have used the entire curriculum in my own classroom, but I became part of the 57% of female teachers who did not return to the classroom for the 2022–2023 academic year (Walker, n.d.). Currently, I am an adjunct instructor at Southside Virginia Community College, and I do use portions of my curriculum in the US History classes I teach there. The differences in knowledge between my students surrounding PEC during the Civil Rights Movement amazes me. Each semester I have had students who personally know some of the people mentioned in the primary sources we use in class, and every semester I have students who grew up in southside Virginia who have never even heard about this history before my class. It would be easy to blame the previous teachers of the ones who do not know about PEC's history, but I was one of those teachers. I did not have the time, access to needed resources, nor bandwidth to find the primary sources and create the lessons until I embarked on the journey to make what I wished had been available to me.

"A Microhistory of Prince Edward County" will not solve all of the issues surrounding the state of education in the United States, but it is a step in the right direction for historians, teachers, and students. Historians outside of K-12 have to take a more active role in helping our K-12 partners; their students will become our students, employees, and supervisors one day. Teachers need free access to comprehensive historical curriculums that encourage students to do history and be historians. Students need to discover the inherent power in understanding our shared past, and that discovery needs to be engaging and relatable to the teenage experience. Primary-source-based lessons have been proven to increase standardized testing scores and student engagement (Reisman, 2011, p. 41), so let's set aside the master narrative and Socratic seminar, occasionally, and do history.

References

Bonastia, C. (2012). *Southern stalemate: Five years without public education in Prince Edward County, Virginia.* University of Chicago Press.

Daugherity, B. J. & Grogan, B. (Eds.). (2019). *A little child shall lead them: A documentary account of the struggle for school desegregation in Prince Edward County, Virginia.* University of Virginia Press.

Green, R. L., & Hofmann, L. J. (1965). A case study of the effects of educational deprivation on southern rural negro children. *The Journal of Negro Education, 34*(3), 327–341. https://www.jstor.org/stable/2294204

Holocaust Museum Houston. (n.d.). The butterfly project. https://butterflies.hmh.org. Accessed on February 5, 2024.

Jeffries, H. K. (Ed.). (2019), *Understanding and teaching the Civil Rights Movement*. The University of Wisconsin Press.

Kobrin, D. (1995). Let the future write the past: Classroom collaboration, primary sources, and the making of high school historians. *The History Teacher, 28*(4). https://www.jstor.org/stable/494638

Maloney, C. (2022). *A microhistory of Prince Edward County, Virginia, 1951–1964: Civil rights curriculum for Virginia's secondary educators*. Master's thesis. Southern New Hampshire University.

Marken, S., & Agrawal, S. K-12 workers have highest burnout rate in U.S. *Gallup*. https://news.gallup.com/poll/393500/workers-highest-burnout-rate.aspx

Moscoviz, L., & Evans, D. K. (2022, March). *Learning loss and student dropouts during the Covid-19 pandemic: A review of the evidence two years after schools shut down*. CGD Working Paper 609. Center for Global Development. https://www.ungei.org/sites/default/files/2022-04/learning-loss-and-student-dropouts-during-covid-19-pandemic-review-evidence-two-years.pdf

Reisman, A. (2011). *Reading like a historian: A document-based history curriculum intervention in urban high schools*. PhD dissertation. Stanford University. https://stacks.stanford.edu/file/druid:by786ht6640/a%20reisman_ReadingLikeaHistorian_CognitionandInstruction.pdf

Robert Russa Moton Museum. (n.d.). Explore galleries. https://motonmuseum.org/visit/#explore-galleries

Sanchez, A. (2019). Rosa did more than sit and Martin did more than dream: Pushing beyond the master narrative with high school students. In H. K. Jeffries (Ed.), *Understanding and teaching the Civil Rights Movement*. The University of Wisconsin Press.

Southern Poverty Law Center. (2024, January 31). Teaching the movement: State of civil rights education in the United States. https://www.learningforjustice.org/sites/default/files/2017-10/Teaching-the-Movement-2011-v2-CoverRedesign-Oct2017.pdf

Titus, J. O. (2011). *Brown's battleground: Students, segregationists, and the struggle for justice in Prince Edward County, Virginia*. The University of North Carolina Press.

Travers, J., & Milgram, S. (1969). An experimental study of the small world problem. *Sociometry, 32*(4), 425-443. https://snap.stanford.edu/class/cs224w-readings/travers69smallworld.pdf

Walker, T. (n.d.). Survey: Alarming number of educators may soon leave the profession. *neaToday*. https://www.nea.org/nea-today/all-news-articles/survey-alarming-number-educators-may-soon-leave-profession. Accessed on February 1, 2024.

CHAPTER 5

A CASE STUDY OF BLACK STUDENTS' EDUCATION AND SOCIALIZATION SINCE PUBLIC SCHOOL CLOSURE IN PRINCE EDWARD COUNTY, VIRGINIA

Jeffrey Carlton Scales
Liberty University, USA

Introduction

The plight of Black youth in America has been a concern for educational and community leaders for over 60 years but came to prominence in recent years with the passage of No Child Left Behind legislation in 2001. In Prince Edward County, Virginia, where public schools were closed from 1959 to 1964 to prevent Blacks and Whites from attending schools together, the public schools there in recent years had difficulty attaining No Child Left Behind federal mandates and Virginia accreditation standards for academic and social success for Black students (U.S. Department of Education, National Center for Education Statistics, 2011). As the only public school system in the United States to close its doors for an extended period of time after the *Brown v. Board of Education* decision, in Prince Edward County the educational recovery of many Black youths are still impacted from the closure, which occurred over 50 years earlier. The educational situation in Prince Edward County was so dire at the time that then–US attorney general Robert Kennedy made the following statement:

> We may observe with much sadness and irony that, outside of Africa, south of the Sahara, where education is still a difficult challenge, the only places known not to provide free, public education are Communist China, North Vietnam, Sarawak, Singapore, British Honduras, and Prince Edward County, Virginia (Smith, 2011, p. 63).

After Prince Edward County decided to close its public schools, Black community leaders in the state of Virginia and across the nation worked diligently to gain equality in American society, especially in the area of public education. During that period in our nation's history, public education was offered by separating races in unequal facilities and substandard instructional materials, yet in Prince Edward County, Virginia, there was refusal to provide even unequal schooling (Bonastia, 2009).

After the *Brown* decision by the Supreme Court, there was a group of White southern Democrats and separatists who fought against school and societal integration. Those individuals started a protest movement called "massive resistance." Massive resistance was executed by many White citizens who were hesitant to the idea of having their children sharing educational facilities, teachers, or materials with Black students and who desired to halt the implementation of the Supreme Court's decision to integrate public schools (Williams, 2004).

In April 1951, 8 years prior to closure of public schools, a student-led strike took place at Robert R. Moton High School in Farmville, Virginia, which was the county seat of Prince Edward County. The 456 students at the all-Black school protested for 2 weeks about separate and very unequal educational opportunities in the county. The students sought to end the overcrowded conditions of the main building of Robert R. Moton High School, which was built to accommodate 180 students, and the three temporary tar paper buildings, which were unheated when first constructed and had no toilet facilities in them (Bonastia, 2012; Stokes et al., 2008). The student strike at the high school did open the eyes of White leaders of the county to the true conditions of the Black high school, and in 1952 those leaders found funding to begin the construction of a new Robert R. Moton High School. With the approval and construction of a new all-Black high school, White leaders anticipated Black leaders would be grateful for the facility and therefore would drop the desegregation lawsuits. With the lawsuits for desegregation continuing through the judicial system, White leaders became more angered because Black citizens were not satisfied with having a separate and equal facility that was their own (Bonastia, 2012; Titus, 2011).

According to a study in 1964 by Robert Green of Michigan State University, of the 1,700 Black school-age children living in Prince Edward County, nearly 1,100 had little to no education during the closure of the county's public schools. He also noted that the impact on those children would possibly have "irreversible effects" (Smith, 1997, p. 7). Of those who did receive educational services, one-quarter of the students ended up attending schools in neighboring counties by living with relatives or moving out of state as far away as North Carolina, Massachusetts, Iowa, and Michigan (Bonastia, 2009; Smith, 2011).

Literature Review

Theoretical Framework

For the purpose of this research, there was a need to establish the foundation of theories that related to the problem of the motivation and socialization factors that impacted Blacks by the closure of public schools. For the Black students and families, there was lost trust in a government that should have protected their educational and social interests as human beings (Heaton, 2008; Titus, 2011). When *Brown v. Board of Education* was decided, "the hope was that desegregated schools would lead to increased educational achievement for African American students as well as improved race relations for the country" (Holland, 2012, p. 101). With the noncompliance of the federal mandate through massive resistance, the movement greatly altered many Black families' motivation in Prince Edward County to seek an education, as they felt that they were written off by White society as not being worth the time to care (Bonastia, 2012; K. Green, 2015; R. L. Green, 1964; Hale-Smith, 1992; Titus, 2011).

Critical Race Theory

The events in Prince Edward County and the closure of public schools there occurred many years prior to the development of critical race theory, but this concept has deep ties that fit this unfortunate episode in our country. This theory encompassing racial changes and the impact of social policies has relevance to this study at the time of public school closure to the current plight of Black student underachievement (Burton et al., 2010). Critical race theory researchers studied the impact of color, ethnicity, and race on inequality and socioeconomic mobility. Their focus was the impact not just on Blacks but also on Asians and non-white Hispanics by looking at how their experiences in American society compared to those of their White counterparts (Burton et al., 2010).

Critical race theory and its connections to racial desegregation, though created in the 1980s, established literature on the social construction of race, ethnicity, and racialization in America. For Blacks, such constructs could be felt with negative perceptions of their existence in American society as equals to those of White citizens (Burton et al., 2010). For those families, earning an education had lost value, and its importance in economical advancement in America led to a struggle of Black citizens to provide for their families due to their lower levels of education. Through the critical race theory perspective, public school closure incorporated the following principles of society at that time: (a) race is a central component of social organizations and systems, including families; (b) racism is institutionalized—it is an ingrained feature of racialized social systems; (c) everyone within racialized social systems may contribute to the reproduction of these systems through social practices; and (d) racial and ethnic identities significantly impact education and socialization (Delgado & Stefancic, 2000, p. xvii).

The Black students of Prince Edward County were denied an education because of the closing of schools, resulting in social, educational, and economic detriments. According to Hale-Smith (1992), who studied Prince Edward County adults impacted by the closing of public schools,

> If there is substantial community membership which distrusts "public officials" because of their unique school experience, then that group may be less likely to be actively involved in community decisions, would probably be less likely to encourage their children to plan for futures in the community, and may, in general, feel disenfranchised (p. 4).

Kozol's (1991) urban example of class and racial disparity was demonstrated in Boston, Massachusetts, public schools when he was a young educator who had started teaching in a poor all-Black elementary school in 1964. He was later recruited to one of the wealthiest schools, which was overwhelmingly White, correlating to critical race theory principles. The facilities, culture, neighborhoods, and students' preparation for learning were drastically different, though the two schools were only miles away from each other. Black children were denied access to adequate materials due to the widespread impoverishment that ran prevalent in their neighborhoods (Dingus, 2006). To further emphasize how racial class in society was interpreted, below is a statement of how Blacks felt about the practice:

> The greatest sense of anger in a number of Black parents that I know is that the obstacles black children face, to the extent that "obstacles" are still conceded, are attributable, at most, to "past injustice"—something dating maybe back to slavery or maybe to the era of official segregation that came to its close during the years from 1954 to 1968—but not, in any case, to something recent or contemporary or on-going (Kozol, 1991, pp. 989–991).

There was truly a need to conduct research as to why such mentalities existed in central Virginia, as most of the literature that had been written had suburban and urban dynamics, which would differ from that of a rural community.

Black Student Academic Achievement

The underlying premise of this case study was to analyze how the closure of public schools in Prince Edward County has impacted the academic and social achievement of Black students there. According to Armor (2006), the *Brown* decision

> ... had little to do with the Black-White achievement gap.... There has been considerable debate over this issue as well, mainly because *Brown* said that segregation harmed Black children's self-esteem and summarized social science evidence about psychological harm of segregation (pp. 40–41).

More recent statistical data on the Black-White achievement gap was conducted by the US Department of Education's National Center for Education Statistics in 2009 through a national sample of over 37,700 high school graduates from private and public schools (2011). In this comparative study, student achievement data from the years 1990, 1994, 1998, 2000, 2005, and 2009 were surveyed to discover the differences between races and ethnicities, gender, and parental educational backgrounds of students from across the nation. Since 1990, there were positive statistics where more high school graduates from all racial and ethnic groups had completed more rigorous school curriculum, earning higher grade point averages and more credits, but in almost every category Black students had the lowest percentages overall. From the survey results, it was discovered that 34% of high school graduates whose parents did not finish high school completed a below-standard curriculum compared to 20% of graduates with parents with college degrees (US Department of Education, National Center for Education Statistics, 2011).

Methodology

Design

This qualitative study utilized the single instrumental case study within a bounded system, which gave the opportunity to conduct a holistic approach to gather thick descriptions for the research (Creswell, 2007). The use of the case study allowed the researcher to develop and investigate in-depth descriptions and address any negative influences that school closure had on Black students' educational achievement the last 2 decades. The qualitative design gave a systematic analysis of past and present events that were developed in great depth through the research process (Berg, 1999; Yin, 2011). Through the development of this identifiable case, there was a valuable opportunity to capture the voices of the research participants, who had relevant details and information that enhanced the strategic importance of this study through personal interviews and the examination of archival records (Stake, 1995; Yin, 2009). The qualitative research design in a logical sequence to connect with the empirical data best served to capture the context of the research through the research questions and conclusions of this moment in history (Yazan, 2015; Yin, 2009). The use of the case study design offered a holistic and biographical research method, which provided the optimum way to explicate the interpretive orientation of the event (Stake, 1995; Yazan, 2015). This case study design was the blueprint for the research as the method that allowed for a more intense understanding and analysis of the interview conversations and interactions with the people most impacted and affected by the closure of public schools (Yin, 2009, 2011). With the current difficulties of Prince Edward County public schools becoming accredited, closing the achievement gap for Black and White students has been a difficult road (US Department of Education, 2010; Virginia Department of Education, 2012; Yin, 2009).

Research Questions

This study was guided by the following three research questions:

1. After public schools in Prince Edward County were reopened in 1964 due to a federal court decision, what were the effects on the educational and social gains of Blacks living in the county at that time?
2. Although this event occurred almost 60 years ago, are there residual effects from the 5-year public school closure still impacting the accomplishments of Black children in Prince Edward County today?
3. In the past decade, Prince Edward County public education has struggled to have Black students close the achievement gap of their White peers and meet federal and state educational mandates. Can this problem be specifically attributed to students' family members (parents, grandparents, guardians, etc.) who lost their education from 1959 to 1964?

Participants

In conducting a single instrumental case study, it was imperative that the sample size remained relatively small in an effort to document rich, lived experiences by the participants in the research. The plan for this case study was to use an initial sample size of 12 participants through purposeful sampling. The actual number of participants in this study was 10, as several potential participants objected to participating, and some were deceased or in poor health. This sampling method was chosen because it was necessary to intentionally select the participant group who provided the best information for the research problem based on their knowledge of the event. For this case study event, it was essential to use purposeful sampling, which was beneficial, as all participants had to have experienced the historical events of school closure or school integration or being raised in families by adults who were not able to receive an education in Prince Edward County (Creswell, 2007).

There was a total of 10 participants in the identified categories:

- Category 1: Former students or parents of those students who were denied an education or had significant knowledge of the closure or reopening of schools in Prince Edward County.
- Category 2: Former students who graduated from segregated Prince Edward County Schools and had significant knowledge of the closure or reopening of schools.
- Category 3: Community leaders with extensive knowledge of the closure of Prince Edward Public Schools or the integration process at the time of the schools' reopening. Their race and gender were not considered for qualification.

The study participants included eight from Category 1, one from Category 2, and one from Category 3.

Participants for the study met the above requirements and were selected after careful analysis of local archives. The documents used included the Prince Edward County Public Schools' school board minutes from 1950 to 1970, a local newspaper, the *Farmville Herald* (which covered the events of the 5-year closures extensively), the personnel and student records of Prince Edward County Public Schools, and the minutes of the Prince Edward County board of supervisors from 1950 to 1970. The prominent names found in those documents were checked to be sure that the individuals were still living to assist with the research.

Procedures

Data collection was not conducted until authorization was given from the Institutional Review Board. Once approval was confirmed, the next step was to follow criterion sampling for those who met the study's criteria. A list was created of potential participants, and research was done to establish ways to communicate with them by personal visit, telephone call, mail, or email. The preferred method for initial communication with the potential participants was through a telephone call, which offered direct explanation as to the purpose of the case study.

A specific telephone format was created to ensure consistency and allow for the development of replicated understanding. If telephone communication was not possible, a face-to-face interaction took place at the homes or facility of those individuals living in the area, which was within a 30-mile radius of Prince Edward County. Those beyond the radius had contact made by family members who explained my efforts. All persons contacted had a letter mailed to them to provide details of the case study and the value of having them assist in the research. The letter had a signature page enclosed to have informed consent of their participation in the study as well as giving the potential participants an opportunity to provide means of electronic communication (e.g., an email address). A confidentiality statement was developed in the initial letter to protect the privacy of participants for their personal information and study responses.

For the retired educators, contact was made initially to the school division's central office regarding the research study and the need for their assistance by identifying those teachers and administrators who met the participation criteria for the study. The study did not find a participant who was teaching currently in Prince Edward County Public Schools who met the criteria for participation. A retired teacher was found who was willing to assist with this case study and had her education delayed by the school closure.

Local community leaders and families directly impacted by the closure of public schools were contacted by telephone to arrange a time for a face-to-face meeting to review the study and its details. Those who agreed to participate were given or mailed the letter and signature page that all other participants received. Once all of the participants had officially verified their willingness to participate, the collection of data began.

Archival documentation was another source of data for this case study. This information was found through public documents that were located at the Prince Edward County Clerk's Office, Prince Edward County Public Schools archives, R. R. Moton Museum, Longwood University Library, and the State Library of Virginia in Richmond. At each location, there was significant information that thoroughly documented the events of the public school closure in Prince Edward County. Specific coverage of school closure was found in the board of supervisors minutes stored at the Prince Edward County Clerk's Office, which was located in the county's administration building. Information from the county's public schools and the school board was found in the archives of the Prince Edward County Public School's central office. All of the research of documents was conducted at those facilities, as those documents were not to be removed from the premises due to their historical importance. The information from the R. R. Moton Museum came from books and documentaries written about the 5-year closure of public schools. Those items were based on the first-hand accounts of local Black civil rights leaders at the time of the school closure or from the perspective of former students who were willing to discuss how the closure impacted their lives. At Longwood University, the library contained an extensive collection of books and local newspaper coverage located in a designated private room for review. The State Library of Virginia offered a variety of record books containing national and state demographics, employment statistics, and economic data that offered relevant information of the time period of public school closure to more recent facts to support the case study research.

Data Collection

In this case study, there was a need to develop a strong background of solid, concrete data for the thick, rich information of this bounded system (Creswell, 2007). Data collection for this case study was conducted through triangulation of event facts by compiling documents, artifacts, and archival records, along with open-ended interviews and focus group interviews that related to the event. The items and information collected provided verbal, numeric, and pictorial data (Creswell, 2007; Yin, 2009, 2011). It was critical to triangulate multiple sources of data to strengthen the evidence for this case study research.

Document Analysis

There was a saturation of the data to validate the results of this case study (Creswell, 2007). Archival records were extremely valuable for this study due to the amount of local, state, and national significance that surrounded the school closure. There were two types of archival records available that were used: (1) public service records, which were made available by local and state governments and school boards, and (2) organizational records from the archives of the local college and museum (Yin, 2009). Once this data were analyzed, there was a thorough review of archival records and historical documentation from the event.

Interviews

A significant amount of research data was collected from the participants through face-to-face interviews, which were structured sessions based on a uniform set of questions. The structured format was chosen to obtain accurate descriptions and interpretations from the participants. The one-on-one interviews consisted of 11 open-ended questions that focused on the perspectives of the former students at the time as well as those of educators and community leaders of Prince Edward County who lived during that time period. Those open-ended and broad questions allowed for the rich descriptions of the voices and experiences of participants (Moustakas, 1994). The perspectives addressed by participants led to strong possibilities for multiple interpretations of the events that occurred due to the closure of public schools (Yin, 2011).

Focus Group

At the conclusion of the individual interviews, a focus group with five participants was coordinated that allowed those who were able to attend to have direct interaction with each other to discuss their perceptions in an open forum. This focus groups offered the advantage of the direct interaction of participants, which, in a small group setting, produced strong feedback with other individuals who had experienced the same events (Creswell, 2007). It was anticipated that the focus group interviews would address research question number 1: "After public schools in Prince Edward County were reopened in 1964 due to massive resistance, what were the effects on the educational and social gains of Blacks living in the county at that time?"

The focus group questions were different from the one-on-one interview questions, and they were revised based on the alignment among the common themes developed from the individual sessions. The anticipated time for the session was not to exceed 1 hour. The focus group session (as were face-to-face interviews) was recorded using one digital and one analog recording device. Those devices were for the verification of participants' statements, with one device serving as the primary recorder and the other as a backup. A notebook was used as a third method of tracking focus group feedback and was designated for the specific use of taking notes during the interview.

Data Analysis

The best technique to analyze the data for this case study was pattern-matching logic, which "compare[s] an empirically based pattern with a predicted one (or with several alternative predictions)" (Yin, 2009, p. 136). The patterns developed assisted in strengthening the internal validity of the study (Yin, 2009). The examination of the data sought to identify two or more patterns that could be displayed in a table for the established pattern based on information analysis (Stake, 1995).

The first step for the data analysis was for me to bracket myself as to any preconceived feelings or ideas about the events of this case study in order to truly understand the experiences of participants and information sources (Creswell, 2007). Using the bracketing method in synthesizing the data allowed for my unbiased views, as any bias could have altered the findings provided from the interviews, focus group, and archival records. It was through this lens that data were analyzed so that the results discovered for this case study did not change.

It was necessary to become familiar with the transcribed interviews and recordings of the one-on-one interviews by listening to the audio repeatedly and establishing common themes that developed and for the accuracy of the transcription following thematic analysis. Research protocols were established in an effort to effectively document the simple repetitions that became evident from the interviews for solid data gathering based on each research question. The discovery of the identified themes from the interview recordings were written out in a designated notebook for accuracy and validity and tallied on the transcription copies. The identified themes were separated in the notebook, which allowed me to better understand the direction the research questions were heading, as inspired by the participants. This procedure was repeated for each interview recording, and the information culminated together as shared theme overviews. As the theme analysis data were accumulated, notations were color-coded to track the added responses until all of the interview recordings were completed. This involved process was done by open coding to reduce the volume of overall data (Creswell, 2007; Merriam, 1991; Stake, 1995).

The same protocols in the previous paragraph were done for the focus group session responses. Along with open coding, memoing was used for the ideas that came from my notations of the face-to-face and focus group interview sessions and their feedback (Creswell, 2007; Stake, 1995). The triangulation process was done by connecting information from the interviews, focus group session, and historical documentation, which allowed for greater combined validation based on the research questions and the findings of the identified themes. The cross-connections of the data allowed a critical view of all assertions of themes and led to uncontestable data description (Stake, 1995).

All interviews were professionally transcribed in order to aide my ability to memo, bracket, and code the events of this single-instrument case study for theme analysis of the identified data. The written format of the spoken conversations of participants assisted me as a visual learner to further increase the validity of the recording, as some points could have been overlooked without this second check. The transcriptions made it easier for me to develop common themes from the verbal dialog. The transcript documents were read no less than two times to allow for a thorough analysis of the questions and participant responses and were analyzed for their connection to the historical documentation used (Yin, 2009, 2011).

An external auditor was requested for greater accuracy of the research data. The external auditor was contacted directly by email and telephone to get an insight into the materials compiled and provided a varied perspective of the analyzed data once they received it. The auditor did not have any connections to the case study event; therefore, their outlook the research was unbiased. The use of an unbiased data reviewer offered a fresh perspective of the retrieved data. The auditor did not have a predisposed view of the event and assisted with better analysis of the transcribed information (Creswell, 2007; Stake, 1995).

Results and Discussion

Participants

The historical research evidence for this case study was conducted through individual interviews from 10 adult participants. Of the participants, eight were former students who had lost some of their education during the 5-year public school closure, one was a former student who graduated from segregated Prince Edward County Schools and had significant knowledge of the closure and reopening of schools, and the final participant was a community leader at the time of the school closures who was involved as a civic leader in the fight to reestablish education in Prince Edward County. All of the participants for this case study were Black. Seven of the participants lived near Farmville. One participant resided in the southern end of Cumberland County near the Farmville town limits. One participant lived about 60 miles west of Farmville. The final participant resided in a city about 65 miles east of Farmville. There were eight men and two women who agreed to participate, and their ages ranged from 63 to 82.

Below are the overviews of key participants. Each participant was identified by a pseudonym to protect their identity for this case study.

Wilson

Wilson was the oldest participant and was the only community leader for this case study. At the time of public school closure in Prince Edward County, he had returned home as a community leader after college. He was a strong activist for racial equality in the public schools in the county and served as a civil rights leader and renowned minister.

Brenda

Brenda was going to enter the eighth grade at R. R. Moton High School at the time public schools were closed. Due to the closure, she was forced to attend school in neighboring Nottoway County, where she had to live with her grandparents for 3 years. Then she returned to the county's Free Schools, where she graduated in 1964. She was a retired educator.

Donald

Donald was supposed to enter the ninth grade when schools closed. He attended segregated schools in Prince Edward County from first grade through eighth grade. As a result of the closure, he did not graduate from high school and moved to New Jersey to work for several years. He went to the local community college and later the local university, where he earned his bachelor's degree. He retired from corrections as a successful warden.

Weldon

Weldon was impacted greatly by the school closure, as he was supposed to have entered first grade in 1959. He did not get any education until 1963, when the Free Schools were opened. When schools in Prince Edward County reopened, he was placed in the fifth grade, although he had no official schooling at the time. He graduated from high school and worked labor-intensive jobs. Later he was a school resource officer in the county where he retired.

Adam

Adam was supposed to have entered the third grade when public schools were closed. He remained in Farmville during the closure and attended the Free Schools when they opened. When public schools reopened, he was placed in the eighth grade. He was a federal employee and a town leader for over 20 years.

Edgar

Edgar was going into the sixth grade when public schools were closed. He continued school in neighboring Appomattox County for 2 years before he returned to Prince Edward County, where he attended the Free School site. After he graduated, he went into the military. He was later employed by a large corporation in a nearby city, where he retired.

Blake

Blake attended schools in Prince Edward County from first grade through fourth grade. At the time of public school closure, he was supposed to be entering the fifth grade. For the first 3 years of closure, he received no formal education, until he moved in 1963 to live with a sister outside the state of Virginia. He later became a school counselor for an urban school district, where he retired.

Two individual interviews were conducted at the Moton Museum, which was the former site of the R. R. Moton High School in Farmville. One interview was conducted at a local Black church in downtown Farmville. Four interviews were held in the homes of the individual participants or a family member. One of the home interviews was a result of the participant's health condition, and the others were more comfortable speaking about the topic in their homes. Two interviews were conducted by telephone due to scheduling difficulties that prohibited a face-to-face interview. One interview was conducted in a conference room at a local school where the participant worked as a substitute teacher. All interviews were recorded and transcribed. Each participant had the opportunity to review their interview responses once they were transcribed to ensure the accuracy of their responses.

Results

Theme Development

The development of this section was based on three research questions:

1. After public schools in Prince Edward County were reopened in 1964 due to a federal court decision, what were the effects on the educational and social gains of Blacks living in the county at that time?
2. Although this event occurred almost 60 years ago, are there residual effects from the 5-year public school closure still impacting the accomplishments of Black children in Prince Edward County today?
3. In past decade, Prince Edward County public education has struggled to have Black students close the achievement gap of their White peers and meet federal and state educational mandates. Can this problem be specifically attributed to students' family members (parents, grandparents, guardians, etc.) who lost their education from 1959 to 1964?

For discovering the depth of the impact the public school closure had on Prince Edward County's Black students in this case study, it was essential to focus on primary archival information from the Prince Edward County board of supervisors' minutes from 1959 to 1970 and the Prince Edward County school board minutes from 1950 to 1969 as primary sources. The data extracted from those sources had to be analyzed in relation to events prior to and after the closure of public schools. The Prince Edward County board of supervisors' minutes offered strong documentation as to the lengths to which White leaders of Prince Edward County would go to completely deny education to all of the children in their county. According to the official minutes, the board of supervisors in Prince Edward County proposed the following:

> The Board of Supervisors of Prince Edward County has refused to approve the Annual Budget for the operation of Public Schools and has refused to approve the Alternative Budget Estimate for Educational Purposes submitted to it by the Superintendent of Public Schools of said County and THE PUBLIC IS HEREBY INFORMED THAT THE BOARD OF SUPERVISORS OF PRINCE EDWARD COUNTY DOES NOT INTEND TO MAKE ANY LEVY OF TAXES OR TO APPROPRIATE ANY MONEY FOR THE OPERATION OF PUBLIC SCHOOLS OF FOR EDUCATIONAL PURPOSES FOR THE YEAR OF 1959–1960 (Supervisors Record #9, 1959–1964, p. 64; Prince Edward County School Board, 1956–1965, p. 119).

The above board of supervisor's proposition was read verbatim by the superintendent to the members of the school board at a meeting the day after the board of supervisors meeting. Without funding, the school board had to cease the operations of public schools immediately and had to develop a press release for the local newspaper and radio station (Prince Edward County School Board, 1956–1965, p. 119).

The impact of this decision was connected to participant Wilson's response from the individual face-to-face interviews. He discussed how the decision to close schools by the board of supervisors was extremely negative for Black students and not as much for Whites. He stated,

> School closing did a job on Black students. Didn't affect many white students, but it did a job on black students … but I can't think of anything else, other than a devastating effect on the students (Black), they were driven from their homeland, went to some places where they excelled and did well. Went to some places where they weren't received real well (Personal communication, September 3, 2016).

At the time of the decision to close schools, there was an immediate impact that was thought to only be a temporary action that would be resolved in a matter of months, but the archival information demonstrated that similar actions by the board of supervisors would continue. In the fall of that year, White leaders opened 15 buildings in the town of Farmville and several areas in Prince Edward County, including churches, which were elements of the beginning of Prince Edward Academy as an all-White private school institution that had not existed prior to the board of supervisors' decision. The academy was accessible to 1,400 of the 2,200 White students of Prince Edward County (Fergeson, 2012).

Ramifications of Lost Educational Opportunity

The decision of Prince Edward board of supervisors in 1959 had long-lasting implications for the county in many facets. The struggle for Black students today harbors sentiments from the former students who were impacted by the closing of public schools in 1959. Participant Brenda, a retired educator, stated:

> It just seems that the stigma was to come to Prince Edward. Now you have a lot of White kids in the school system and a lot of the Black kids are being pushed aside and White kids achieving.... Those are the kids (Black students) that are coming from homes that the parents did not get a formal education. They struggle (Personal communication, September 5, 2016).

Another common theme from the interviews and focus group discussions was the lost academic opportunities of former students due to the school closure. The closing of schools altered their lives, but they were able to overcome that detriment. Several participants did not go to college as a result. Participant Weldon stated:

> When I graduated from high school, I was offered three scholarships. One was to Longwood College, first year for basketball, St. Benedict College, and Mitchell College. I turned them all down. I knew I wasn't going to pass academically. I knew athletically I could have competed, but academically it was no way I could have done it. A part of me always wondered what it would be like if I had the additional education (Personal communication, September 13, 2016).

The two experiences described above are representative of those of many capable Blacks in Prince Edward County whose lives could have been different had their education not been disrupted. They are a small sample of Black citizens who probably could have had different life outcomes. The participants of these interviews and focus group were able to have successful lives and careers, but they know many classmates and relatives who were not as fortunate.

Weldon saw the negative impact on student achievement for Blacks in the county being based on the racial demographics of the teaching staff, which is currently predominantly White. He stated:

> I think today that's killing our system. I have nothing against females, but White females and some Black females cannot teach our Black males.... I know for a fact, I think its two Black male teachers at the middle school.... They are really forsaking the Black males at Prince Edward.... They're not going to see a male, a Black male until they get to high school (Personal communication, September 13, 2016).

Brenda, Adam, Donald, Weldon, and Edgar remembered two particular Black families in the county who had 22 and 18 children, respectively. None of the children of those two families ever graduated from school, as they stayed on the family farms to help their parents raise the family and support their parents. Participant Adam presented this concern by stating:

> Those years out of school did some damage. I look at the XXXXX family. They had 22 kids. You think about it, 22 kids that didn't go to school. XXXXX, would tell the story of how they used to make it, twenty some (thing) kids in one house. When schools closed down, they worked on a farm and did this and that back in the day. The XXXXX family was the same way. I think it was 18 of them. So it was an impact right there (Personal communication, September 21, 2016).

Those 40 children were examples of Black families who put their survival ahead of having their children earn their education. Fortunately, all 40 of those children were able to be successful as adults at mostly menial jobs, although one of them was a successful restaurant owner in Farmville for many years.

Several participants felt that the school closing was so long ago that there was less of a chance that their classmates would have children in the county schools currently. As noted in the previous paragraphs, though, the participants knew large numbers of Black families who had limited education at the time of the school closings, with grandchildren and great-grandchildren currently in Prince Edward County Schools. Participant Adam commented that he felt that the children and grandchildren of the Black citizens with limited education would not have their education affected today. He said:

> A lot of the troublemakers now are not the children of the people that were impacted by the schools closing. They are like the great-great-grandchildren or nephews or something. It's hard to say if they were impacted because it was so far down the line (Personal communication, September 21, 2016).

Weldon viewed it differently and said the impacted families would put less value on doing well in school. He stated:

> It's through the generations. Some of them, well a lot of them made it okay (without an education). Some of their families were educated. A lot of their parents say they made it with no education. So you [the child] can do it too (Personal communication, September 13, 2016).

Weldon's opinion was shared other participants and demonstrated a sad thought process that many families possessed that led some of the current generation of students to not excel academically in school.

Most of the participants felt that the reopening of schools as desegregated educational facilities had the greatest impact on the county. Seven of the participants agreed that having the schools reopened was good but did not see immediate change racially. Blake felt that the integration of public schools was a mistake. He stated:

> The schools should have stayed the way it was to me.... The schools should have never been integrated. Integration was going to come anyway. When you try to force something on people that really messed Prince Edward up, because they were trying to force integration (Personal communication, September 23, 2016).

In conclusion, thankfully, all of the interview participants had been able to overcome the atrocities of the public school closure in their lives. Each one had different experiences after 1959, but all of them had the common spirit to succeed in life and were able to clearly express their feelings about the 5-year closure of schools in their home county.

Theoretical Implications

The implications of this case study and the events that occurred as a result of the 5-year closure of Prince Edward County Public Schools and its extremely limited integration effort to reopen schools can have far-reaching effects on similar rural communities with demographics of Blacks or other minority populations over 25%. Rural school divisions could consider using this study to address past wrongs in their communities, and the data presented could be analyzed for current citizens' feelings that may not be articulated openly in order to avoid another potential episode of prolonged educational denial. The importance of such understanding as to the impact or the implied feelings of citizens who had their educations decimated by the actions of local government would have lasting benefits toward more harmonious communities across our country.

Empirical Implications

There were rural areas in our nation that have had racial episodes that impacted Black citizens negatively and could have had lingering effects. The primary difference is that no other locale affected a group of people to the magnitude of the events in this case study. For example, several school divisions in the state of Virginia closed public schools for a year to prevent Black and White children from going to school together, but only Prince Edward County chose to close for an extended period of time, which brought national government attention. The actions and its effects were not reversible for those individuals who could not go to school when schools were closed. For those Black citizens in Prince Edward County who overcame the lengthy closure with little to no schooling (compared to those who had the means of not losing their education), the trials that were overcome from all perspectives can offer a great amount of input for those researchers who are willing to research the case study's true direct impact.

Practical Implications

Beyond schools, sociologists who research racial impacts on society would be able to use this case study to understand the impact of long-held negative feelings by people in communities who have been treated unfairly. Negative episodes in societal decisions need immediate intervention so that there will be no festering wounds that would exist in impacted communities.

In the field of political science, the events of school closings have had direct relevance to racial and political injustices that have long-lasting effects and cause resistance by some citizens, especially minorities. From time to time, historical events such as the incidents that occurred in Prince Edward County have led to manifested negative racial perceptions and actions that have lingered among communities along racial lines. Having an in-depth understanding of the significance of school closings for Black citizens can contribute to a better understanding of what is needed to resolve educational concerns such as closing the achievement gap or raising minority graduation rates.

Conclusion

It was surprising to discover that the Black citizens affected by the school closures did not feel that there was a correlation between the Prince Edward County school closure from 1959 to 1964 and the success of Black students in the county schools today. This case study should hopefully dispel the perception and myth that the public school closure is still impacting their

Black students today from being successful and socially relevant. The limitations discovered while acquiring participants for this study made it difficult to have a stronger sample to get more diversified responses. There were no participants who were not successful economically and socially within the county. As for future research, there is truly a need to gain an understanding from the perspective of over 800 White students who lost their education during the closure. It is an element that needs to be addressed before those who experienced it are deceased or physically unable to participate. Another future study could analyze the impact of the relocation of Black students to other localities, whether within the state of Virginia or out of state, for their educations, who never returned to Prince Edward County to live. Many of those who never returned were extremely successful, and the local area never had the chance to have them as an influence or role model for the Black youth of the community.

References

Armor, D. J. (2006). Brown and Black-White achievement. *Academic Questions, 19*(2), 40–46.
Berg, B. L. (1999). *Qualitative research methods for the social sciences.* Allyn & Bacon.
Bonastia, C. (2009). White justifications for school closings in Prince Edward County, Virginia, 1959–1964. *Du Bois Review, 6*(2), 309–333.
Bonastia, C. (2012). *Southern stalemate: Five years without public education in Prince Edward County, Virginia.* The University of Chicago Press.
Burton, L. M., Bonilla-Silva, E., Ray, B., Buckelew, R., & Freeman, E. H. (2010). Critical race theories, colorism and the decade's research on families of color. *Journal of Marriage and Family, 72,* 440–459.
Creswell, J. W. (2007). *Qualitative inquiry & research design: Choosing among five approaches* (2nd ed.). Sage.
Delgado, R., & Stefancic, J. (2000). *Critical race theory: The cutting edge* (2nd ed.). Temple University Press.
Dingus, J. E. (2006). "Doing the best we could": African American teachers' counter story on school desegregation. *The Urban Review, 38*(3), 211–233.
Fergeson, L. S. (2012). *The Moton school story: Children of courage.* Eastern National.
Green, R. L. (1964). *The educational status of children in a district without public schools.* Cooperative Research Project No. 2321. Bureau of Educational Research. Michigan State University.
Green, K. (2015). *Something must be done about Prince Edward County: A family, a Virginia town, a civil rights battle.* HarperCollins Publishers.
Hale-Smith, M. E. (1992). *The early effects of educational disruptions on the belief systems and educational practices of adults.* PhD dissertation. Michigan State University. ProQuest Dissertations and Theses. http://media.proquest.com.ezproxy.liberty.edu:2048/media/pq/classic/doc/745218441
Heaton, P. (2008). Childhood educational disruption and later life outcomes: Evidence from Prince Edward County. *Journal of Human Capital, 2*(2), 154–187.

Holland, M. M. (2012). Only here for the day: The social integration of minority students at a majority White high school. *Sociology of Education, 85*(2), 101–120.
Kozol, J. (1991). *Savage inequalities*. Crown Publishing Group.
Merriam, S. B. (1991). *Case study research in education: A qualitative approach*. Jossey-Bass.
Moustakas, C. (1994). *Phenomenological research methods*. Sage.
Prince Edward County School Board. (1956, July 2–1965, June 14). *School Board Minutes—Book V. Prince Edward County School Board Office Archives*.
Smith, R. C. (1997). Prince Edward County: Revisited and revitalized. *Virginia Quarterly Review, 73*(1), 1–27.
Smith, R. C. (2011). Prince Edward County and racial redemption. *Virginia Social Science Journal, 46*, 57–82.
Stake, R. E. (1995). *The art of case study research*. Sage.
Stokes, J. A., Wolfe, L., & Viola, H. J. (2008). *Students on strike: Jim Crow, civil rights, Brown and me*. National Geographic.
Supervisors Record #9 Prince Edward County. (1959–1964). *Prince Edward County Clerk's Office*.
Titus, J. O. (2011). *Brown's battleground: Students, segregationists, & the struggle for justice in Prince Edward County, Virginia*. The University of North Carolina Press.
US Department of Education. (2010). *No Child Left Behind: Elementary and Secondary Education Act*. http://www2.ed.gov./policy/elsec/leg/esea02/index.html
US Department of Education, National Center for Education Statistics. (2011). *The nation's report card: America's high school graduates*. http://nces.ed.gov/nationsreportcard/pdf/studies/2011462.pdf
Virginia Department of Education. (2012). *Prince Edward County high school report card*. https://p1pe.doe.virginia.gov/reportcard/report.do?
Williams, J. (2004). The 1964 Civil Rights Act. *Human Rights, 31*(3), 6–8.
Yazan, B. (2015). Three approaches to case study methods in education: Yin, Merriam, Stake. *The Qualitative Report, 20*(2), 134–152. http://www.nova.edu/ssss/QR/QR20/2/yazan1.pdf
Yin, R. K. (2009). *Case study research: Design and method* (4th ed.). Sage.
Yin, R. K. (2011). *Qualitative research from start to finish*. The Guilford Press.

CHAPTER 6

ADDRESSING SILENCE: ORAL HISTORY AS A TOOL TO TEACH DIFFICULT HISTORY

Rory Dunn
Virginia Commonwealth University, USA

Introduction

Once you were in public school and you were a certain age you knew about the Academy. Even if you weren't thinking about it you were thinking about it. It was kind of subconsciously embedded in your head that there were White kids that were maybe coming from that school that are going here, or that there were White kids that are fleeing to that school if they didn't like it here (F. Moseley II, personal communication, March 7, 2022).

What Frank Moseley II described in the opening moments of our interview was a phenomenon known as "White flight," where parents of White students sent their children to private, White-only schools to avoid the threat of desegregated public schools. Frank's omnipresent awareness of Prince Edward Academy was a long-lasting scar from a trauma endured by the previous generation of students in Prince Edward County. Frank's mother, Rita Moseley, was one of the students who was shut out of public schools during the infamous Prince Edward County school closures from 1959 to 1964.

Virginia played a considerable role in the movement known as "Massive Resistance," where legislators, civil servants, and everyday people worked to resist the ruling made in *Brown v. Board*. Among the states that participated in Massive Resistance, Virginia took the most extreme approach.

At the behest of figures like state senator Garland Gray and US senator Harry Byrd, concrete plans to implement Massive Resistance took shape. Tuition grants, garnished from public funds and fundraised from local drives and donors, were provided to White families who wished to send their students to private, segregated schools (Bonastia, 2012; Titus, 2011). Prince Edward Academy, the school mentioned by Frank, was one such White-flight school. Most damaging, however, was that funding was denied to public schools who attempted to integrate. For those in Prince Edward County, this meant that families who were categorically excluded from White-flight schools, and those who could not afford to send their kids to school, were effectively out of luck. If they wanted their children to go to public school, they would have to leave the county. Many families did not have the resources or social networks to send their children to attend public school elsewhere. The public schools would remain closed in Prince Edward County for 5 years.

In the wake of the COVID-19, school closures, and the subsequent reported educational losses, the damage from the Prince Edward County school closures seems unfathomable. Robert Green, an educational researcher from Michigan State University, and later a significant member of the Southern Christian Leadership Conference, conducted a study in 1964 to examine the learning loss of the students who were locked out of schools. Green and Hoffmann (1965) compared scores from youths in Prince Edward County to those in adjacent counties; the results of the comparison were dire. Students who had lived through the closure and had attended little to no school performed significantly worse than their peers on several metrics. A follow-up study by Green and Morgan (1969) corroborated the severity of the educational loss.

By the 1980s, Frank was a student at Prince Edward High School, attending school in the very county that had shut his mother out. Prince Edward Academy still stood as a perpetual reminder to the community of the closures. In 1978, the Internal Revenue Service issued new guidelines to address the surge in White-flight schools (Drake, 1979). Prince Edward Academy remained indignant in the face of the changes; an article from the *Clarion-Ledger* reported that the segregationist lawyer for the school stated,

> We're discriminatory as hell.... We're g—d— if we're going to tell everyone that we were hypocrites all those years. Fundamentally, we believe blacks deserve a different type of education than whites. We strongly believe whites among whites and blacks among blacks get a better education ("All-white academy," 1985, p. 3C).

The academy lost its tax-exempt status. Years of financial hardship eventually led the academy to begrudgingly eliminate discriminatory language from its admissions policy; nominally, the school had "integrated," but Frank, his peers, and members of the public noted that the school still retained the values espoused by their lawyer.

For Frank, there still existed a vast cohort of parents and students who would rather pay money to send their kids to a de facto White-only private school than to partake in a desegregated classroom. He noted:

> Segregation was still strong and alive up until probably they changed the name to Fuqua. Why they started it? In my opinion they did it only because they knew it had financial incentives for doing so. Whether they were legal or whatnot. They saw the advantage of having diversity and getting credits for having diversity in their private school. I guess the committee switched over to a charter? I don't know what it is. But they did something, and we knew about it (F. Moseley II, personal communication, March 7, 2022).

Positionality and Lived Experience

When I was hired to teach social studies in a county adjacent to Prince Edward County, I was thrilled. I was a fresh graduate, and I was eager to cut my teeth teaching in a rural community, one that I thought reflected a similar educational environment to the one where I grew up. I felt particularly prepared to teach history. I had studied history throughout my undergraduate experience and familiarized myself with the standards of learnings for the classes I was to teach. Even though I thought I had made efforts to prepare for my first year of teaching, I was blissfully ignorant of the region's tumultuous past. Little within the standards or my undergraduate classes revealed much about the "Long Civil Rights" movement or provided complexity beyond the messianic narratives of figures who have become larger than life in the American public consciousness; in history instruction across the nation, household names like Martin Luther King Jr., Rosa Parks, and Booker T. Washington remain indelibly linked to exceptional activism (Woodson, 2016).

When I first taught about the Civil Rights Movement, I was surprised by the reactions of my students. Many of them rolled their eyes, loudly stated their disinterest, or disengaged when we covered the Selma to Montgomery marches, the speeches of Martin Luther King Jr., but especially when we touched on *Brown v. Board* and a relevant footnote in the standards of learning standards: "Massive Resistance." I thought a history of progress and resistance to oppression would be engaging. At the time I did not know that this narrative was deeply flawed. American progress toward freedom has never been linear and has frequently backslid, something that historian Eric Foner (1998, 2015) has written about.

Beyond its inaccuracy, the narrative of consistent American progress toward freedom was disconnected from the context of where I was teaching. I remember talking to one of my peers in the history department about the unit, a local whose family had long-standing roots in the county. When I recounted my frustrations, he just chuckled and told me to "do my homework." When schools shuttered in March of 2020 and I found myself sequestered at home, I worked to do just that. I started a master's program in history so that I could teach dual-enrollment classes for my students and bolster my content knowledge. During the program, I took time to learn more about Massive Resistance and the closures that had taken place just next door to where I was teaching. I was stunned. I was born and raised in Virginia, attended K–12 schools in Virginia, studied history at a Virginia state school, yet Massive Resistance was never meaningfully covered in any curriculum I had taken part in.

Reflecting on my pedagogy from that first year, I am ashamed. I was frustrated by the lack of engagement from my students but had not considered the personal nature of the history I was trying to cover. I did not consider my status as a community outsider. Some of my students in my classroom were the descendants of victims of the closures. Some were the descendants of perpetrators. The way that I taught the Civil Rights Movement was unyoked from the experience of their families, a facsimile of a national rhetoric of progress. Worse, it obfuscated stories of trauma and pain and, most importantly, narratives of resilience and success.

In 2021, I conducted an oral history project with the goal of looking at how the trauma of the school closures manifested both in those who experienced the closures and in their children. That was how I met Frank and Rita and came to know their stories. Despite both enduring considerable trauma from the closures and their radial effects, both Frank's and Rita's stories are exemplary narratives of considerable resilience, an area of research that remains largely unexamined regarding the school closures. Williams's (2013) groundbreaking dissertation was among the first literature to examine narratives of resilience and success about the closures. His phenomenological case study examined several participants who endured the closures and went on to become exemplars of professional and academic success. Craig (2010) similarly covered narratives of resilience from several community members of Prince Edward County, contrasting Black resilience to White resistance.

Frank and Rita became highly educated, achieving academic success, and both became stalwart advocates for education. Frank is now the Chief Executive Officer of a nonprofit, the Social Education for Economic Development Initiative, which seeks to pool community resources and provide opportunities for adult learning in civics, financial literacy, and history. Rita—the author of many books, including *No School* and *Silence Broken After 50 Years*—remains a frequent speaker at local schools, where she shares her story.

When I taught about the Civil Rights Movement that year, I completely redesigned my unit; a focal point of the overarching narrative became the local effects of the closures. Rita's and Frank's stories drove the inquiry. It was a difficult unit. I found that my students were engaged, but the class conversations were raw and painful. We questioned the simple narrative of progress by framing it with local stories of what was lost and gained. We discussed what was next by linking the past to the present: discussion covered reparations, the Black Lives Matter movement, and what it meant to be a citizen in a community that had inflicted hurt and been hurt.

The goal of this conceptual chapter is to outline what I learned through this process, to write what I wish I could have read before beginning my first year of teaching social studies. How can oral history be used as a tool for accessing silenced narratives and addressing difficult knowledge? I will engage with theories of narrative silences and difficult knowledge/difficult history using my oral history work with the Prince Edward County school closures. The chapter ends with suggestions for teachers working where historical trauma has fractured communities.

Methodology

Oral History

It is important to note that oral history is not research. Research involves a systematic investigation with the purpose of creating generalizable knowledge. Oral history seeks to help place people's experiences within a larger social and historical context. As a result of this difference in goals, oral history interviews differ from those typically conducted in educational research. In qualitative educational research, an interview protocol is shared with and approved by an Institutional Review Board before the interview process. In oral history work, the interview protocol is something that can be designed collaboratively with the interviewee: It is an exercise in shared power, a deference to lived experience, a chance to provide counter-narrative a platform. Before the interview, the interviewer and interviewee establish protocol for how the conversation will be recorded, with whom it will be shared, and where the transcript and recording will be stored. During the interview, the interviewee has the power to direct the flow of the conversation; they determine what is and is not worth sharing. While oral history work is exempt from Institutional Review Board processes, oral historians have established their own code of best practices and ethical considerations. Special considerations about the power dynamic between the interviewer and the interviewee must be made, and trust and transparency between parties must be established and preserved throughout the process (Kyriakoudes, 2023).

The oral history work included in this chapter originates from a larger project (Dunn, 2022). A combination of primary and secondary sources was used as prompts during the interviews to direct lines of questioning and to tap into public memory surrounding significant community members and events. The interviewees signed written disclosure forms and were orally informed of the project's purpose. Discussions were held regarding the storage, publication, and audience of the interviews; these conversations led to adjustments in the disclosure forms to reflect interviewee concerns. The conversations with the community members were recorded on a high-quality audio recorder and transcribed by hand by the author. The software *OTranscribe* was used in the transcription process, as it is locally hosted on the interviewer's device and therefore is inaccessible to third parties or the software developers. This ensured that the interviews were confidential in accordance with the privacy agreements outlined in the disclosure forms. This step was of the utmost importance given the difficulties in establishing trust with the interviewees. The thematic question set used in the interview was adapted from the life history set provided by the Center for Oral History Research based out of the University of California, Los Angeles (*Oral Histories*; see the Appendix). Oral history interviews are fluid and collaborative: Not every question was asked, and questions were brought up that are not reflected in the original set of questions.

Theory

Purposeful Silence

Silence, gaps, and narrative omissions have a peculiar effect on us. Just as we are drawn to stories and narratives, we are also drawn to the negative: what isn't discussed, what is missing, and the tantalizing question of *why* something isn't there. My work with Frank and Rita reified a trend about the school closures that is shared among other groups who have experienced considerable historical trauma: silence. Silence was pervasive, both within the community that had perpetrated the misdeeds and in those who endured them. Much of the literature on silence and intergenerational memory stems from research into survivor memory of the Holocaust. In one such work, Eva Hoffman (2004) reflected on the nature of second-generation memory, trauma, and silence through analysis of her own family life and the lives of her peers. Hoffman recalled:

> But the general silence on the subject, the lack of interest, meant that in many families, the secret past became even more of a secret, that the different kind of silence prevailing among survivors became reinforced, that the children,

as they were growing up, were thrown into greater confusion and emotional isolation. The latency period burrowed right back into families and minds, reinforcing the psychology of suppression, delaying the reckoning with the past and its aftereffects (p. 94).

Hoffman's work provided insight into the multitude of reasons for the silence of survivors: a lack of interest from external parties, fear of further oppression, and a desire to leave the past behind. Hoffman also alluded to the tangible costs of these silences: For the next generation, this can manifest as confusion and emotional isolation. In one such instance, Frank remembered playing on the playground next to Prince Edward Academy:

> I remember telling my mom she was like "Where have you been?" "Oh, we were up there playing." "You were playing where?" And she just kind of freaked out! "Don't you know that you're not supposed to be over there? That's the Academy's!" It was like an alarm went off, like I had done something wrong. I was like "What are you talking about? I was just on the playground." You know, I didn't understand (personal communication, March 7, 2022).

Just as there are varied reasons for victims of trauma to maintain silence, there are reasons for perpetrator silence. Scott Ellsworth's (1982) investigation into the Tulsa Race Massacre examined one such case by looking at two oral traditions: one continued by the White Tulsans who perpetrated the violence and one that was continued by the Black Tulsans who endured it. Ellsworth found that Black Tulsans discussed the massacre: For the community who endured the racial violence, rebuilding became a point of community pride and Black resilience. Meanwhile, White Tulsans who participated in the massacre were reluctant to discuss their role as perpetrators. Mediating their decision was concern "about the city's image ... that young, beautiful Tulsa was a city bound for glory" (Ellsworth, 1982, p. 120). Shame, incrimination, and image were powerful motivators that suppressed the spread of the Tulsa Race Massacre.

The dichotomous nature of perpetrator silence and the silences of the affected reveals a stark truth about how we engage with history. Historical narratives are constructs that are influenced by the societal structures of power; what we engage with in the classroom is often a reflection of which narratives best serve that structure. In his seminal work on narrative silences, Trouillot (1995) asserted that in interpreting narratives,

> ... what matters most are the process and conditions of production.... Only a focus on that process can uncover the ways in which the two sides of historicity intertwine in a particular context. Only through that overlap can we discover the differential exercise of power that makes some narratives possible and silences others (p. 25).

In my interview with Frank, he recalled his frustration with that narrative control. When Frank was in school, options to discuss the history that divided his immediate community were limited, even among the contexts where they would have been natural to discuss. Frank speculated on the disconnect between what he learned in his history classrooms and his lived experience:

> Frank: It wasn't something that was really celebrated or you know brought up during Black History Month. It wasn't something that was a common thread in the overarching history of landmark decisions.
>
> Rory: Things that you would learn about in school history class?
>
> Frank: Right, exactly.
>
> Rory: So why do you think that thread wasn't there. Why was that not talked about?
>
> Frank: Well, it's a lot of embarrassment.
>
> Rory: From the White people that did the closings?
>
> Frank: Indeed (personal communication, March 7, 2022).

Oral history is an excellent tool for accessing local narratives that are obfuscated, especially those that embody struggle, resilience in the face of oppression, and challenges to master narratives. Empowerment and voice lie at the heart of oral history work: In the case of the Prince Edward County school closures, the narratives of Frank and Rita go beyond the structural explanations for Massive Resistance. Instead of looking at state politicians and their plans for resisting integration, their stories are steeped in local grievances, successes, and community weaknesses and strengths. Incorporating these stories into the classroom is powerful: It is history that is intimately linked to the lived experiences of the students. At the same time, these stories are painful to confront. What does it mean to engage with a community trauma in the classroom?

Difficult Knowledge

Difficult knowledge, first theorized by Britzman (1998), is a psychoanalytic term that engages with how students deal with conflict, both internal and external, especially when those students are confronted with narratives of violence. The late Roger Simon (2014), a pioneer on the work of difficult knowledge in the field of education, noted that "at the heart of the matter regarding questions of difficult knowledge is the provocation of affect, and most importantly, affect's relation to the instigation and possibilities of thought" (p. 7). Entertaining difficult knowledge necessitates engaging with knowledge that makes us uncomfortable; it requires us to consider our assumptions, to relate with material we wish to shirk away from. As a result, engaging with difficult knowledge is unsettling and inflammatory by design: for students with links to perpetrators, guilt, shame, and disorientation are powerful incentives of avoidance. For those with links to those affected, engagement can be a painful reminder of past trauma. The costs of such avoidance can be high. Simon (2014) noted:

> Critics have argued that such a use of memory has done little more than encourage a form of abjection enacted through identification with either victims or those who have sought to prevent or contest victimization. Such identifications result in placing the self at a comfortable, distinguishing distance from those rendered as malefic, malicious perpetrators of injustice, eviscerating the force of memory for rethinking how one might alter the way one lives in the present (p. 3).

Historical distance can be sanitizing and unengaging: It unyokes us from current conditions that often have linkages to past trauma and removes the impetus for corrective action. Garrett (2017) argued that pedagogy that employs difficult knowledge orients us toward action and responsibility: "Social education is supposed to be the location for the cultivation of a sense of place in the world among others with whom we share concern and responsibility" (p. 35). Therefore, difficult knowledge provides not just a framework for addressing past trauma and links to current events but also an analysis of the structural mechanisms that lead to the perpetuation of future injustices. History is an ideal medium for approaching difficult knowledge: after all, it is through earnest study of the past that we can cultivate place and foment collective action. It is for this reason that difficult knowledge has been integrated with growing frequency in history education research.

Difficult History

Since the advent of difficult knowledge to educational research, scholars have attempted to tackle how teachers and students engage with difficult knowledge in the form of *difficult history,* a concept that has been heavily theorized (Garrett, 2017; Gross & Terra, 2018; Stoddard, 2022; Zembylas, 2014) and that is garnering growing empirical support (Harris et al., 2022). The educational theory on difficult history is varied but shares common threads across authors. Zembylas (2014) theorized a framework for difficult history that situates the "psychosocial affect ... because it directs attention to the social and political norms that are entangled with our everyday habits or differential recognition of others, and especially how these norms and habits are perceived corporally" (p. 403). To complicate the psychoanalytic roots of difficult history, Zembylas (2014) incorporated concepts of Judith Bulter's work: vulnerability and action orientation. Garrett (2017) theorized a difficult history that "invite[s] us to think about the ways in which living in the world exposes our vulnerability to each other and how that vulnerability is political, civic, historical, economic and geographic issue" (p. 46). Perhaps the most concrete definition of *difficult history* has emerged from the work of Gross and Terra (2018), who captured the affective, disruptive, and insurgent elements of difficult history through five criteria:

1. Difficult history is central to the history of the nation.
2. Difficult histories challenge broadly accepted versions of the past.
3. Difficult histories connect past problems to those that exist in the present.
4. Difficult histories involve violence, usually collective or state sanctioned.
5. Difficult histories create disequilibria that causes those that learn them to question their assumptions or beliefs (p. 4).

These criteria are a useful litmus test for determining whether a history is "difficult," a designation that is contextual and difficult to meet. So, does the history of the Prince Edward County school closures constitute a difficult history? For the context of where I was teaching, I believe so. The fight for and against integration in the county is intimately central to a core national narrative of US history: the narrative of progress toward freedom (Foner, 1998, 2015). The closures represent a significant challenge to this narrative of consistent progress toward freedom. The stories behind the closures have significant linkages from the past to the present in the form of the loss of education and institutional trust (Dunn, 2022). The closures are a clear example of state-sanctioned harm. Most importantly, the inclusion of the history of the closures leads us to question basic myths about American society: that the effects of *Brown v. Board* have long secured a post-racial American milieu. In our interview, Frank recalled engaging with the difficult history of the school closures. He noted:

> I think I was inspired by what I learned when my uncle came down and started talking about his experience with the school closing. I started doing some research on it on my own. [My mother] started introducing me to people, like Reverend Griffin. I didn't know who these people were sometimes. I was like okay, cool cool, alright. She started telling me more and more about these things. I started to understand things like free lunch and schools in churches and what they had to do in order to survive during that period of time. That is

what gave me the understanding of what I could do as a grassroots organization, being able to come to Richmond and start using social education as a means of self-education (personal communication, March 7, 2022).

Frank's engagement with the difficult history of the closures was transformative. The difficult history was a linkage to the past but provided a framework for action in the present: a goal to address past wrongs through grassroots organization. For my students, the narratives of Frank and Rita were histories of profound hope: a rejection of the national narrative of progress but an endorsement of the efficacy of community-oriented action. The incorporation of this oral history into my classroom was deeply contextual and something that was locally driven. But what happens when difficult history does not access community trauma in the way it is intended?

Stoddard (2022) indicated in their theoretical review of difficult history that there are three implications for current work with difficult history. First, the perceptions and role of teachers, especially regarding their moral positioning, have implications for teacher preparation and development. Second, the literature on difficult history has largely encouraged the role of emotion in unsettling and processing difficult history. Third, when engaging in difficult history with students, context and identity matter (p. 391). Stoddard's (2022) last point is particularly important; he noted that if

> ... the strength of this theory is the ability to attempt to make sense of how people encounter, become unsettled by, and then work through an encounter with representations of social trauma. One key weakness ... is that it does not readily generalise or fully take into account social and cultural contextual factors for this meaning making (p. 395).

How can we be sure that difficult history is properly contextualized, that it resonates with students in such a way that it leads them to be unsettled, to question assumptions?

Oral History: Accessing Local Difficult History

Just as oral history work is an ideal medium for accessing silenced narratives, it is also ideal for accessing the most contextual histories. If concerns about the practice of difficult history relate to the specific contexts and cultural nuances of particular locales, what better tool to situate difficult history than the narratives of those locales? Students' degrees of separation from the oral history of their community are significantly reduced compared to national narratives. Research on the use of oral history in the classroom has reported numerous pedagogical benefits such as increased student engagement (Dayton-Wood et al., 2012) and a deeper understanding of how historians conduct their work (Dutt-Doner et al., 2016). Johnson and Mason (2017), in their study of undergraduate students who practiced oral history surrounding the Civil Rights Movement, indicated that the pedagogical tool of oral history facilitated race talk and prompted students to interact with feelings of guilt, concepts like structural racism, and social action.

Implications for Practice and Research

For those who work in communities where historical trauma is particularly palpable, oral history may be an excellent pedagogical tool for accessing narrative silences, building engagement with content material, and teaching students to engage with difficult history. Oral history is particularly useful when silence obfuscates narratives of trauma and resilience in lieu of simple narratives of progress in places where there is "silence, indirect revelations, felt scars, the passage of pain" (Hoffman, 2004, p. 251). Attending to the theories of purposeful silence through oral history work might orient students to consider multiple perspectives in history, the constructed nature of historical narratives, and the role of power in determining what histories we are exposed to. There are considerable overlaps between the spaces where narrative silences occur and where difficult history begins. Using oral history to situate difficult history to local contexts might mitigate some of the concerns brought up by Stoddard (2022)—namely that difficult history must consider the context and cultural meaning-making that may be specific to local contexts. History that is sourced from one's own community might forge a stronger affective link and anchor student inquiry in the disequilibria that makes difficult history what it is: an opportunity for students to engage with trauma, question their assumptions, and reorient themselves in a pedagogy of affect.

There is a need for empirical studies that examine the role of oral history in facilitating student engagement with difficult history. Such studies would provide invaluable information on how oral history might lead students to engage authentically with difficult history. Such work might also provide insights into how localizing difficult history could mitigate concerns about the efficacy of difficult history in appropriately achieving a state of disequilibria where contextual and cultural meaning-making may influence interaction with source material in unexpected ways.

Conclusion

As a teacher, my work in oral history paid dividends for my students and radically changed my pedagogy. It replaced a sanitized version of history, disjointed from the reality of my students' community, with a more human one, and it made me approach the Civil Rights Movement from a new lens.

Engaging with the stories of Frank and Rita in the classroom was painful: students talked about their family history and engaged with conversations about guilt, shame, reparations, and reconciliation. It can seem natural to avoid this discomfort, but we owe it to our students to teach difficult history; linking past injustices to the present and helping students acquire the apparatus to question assumptions and simple narratives provides students with the impetus to address them. As a final note, consider one last excerpt from my interview with Frank. In recalling this conversation Frank had with Rita as a college student, Rita imparts a perennial piece of wisdom:

> I still really understood what college was about, or why it was so important that I went. And so when [my parents] sat me down and asked me about what I was going to do after graduating high-school … [my mother's] like "Do you want to go to college?" And I was just like "I don't know, not really." And she was like, "Well you know, we really never got the chance to go to college, you know why?" And I was like "No." "I told you before that your dad didn't graduate high school. Yeah, well back when we were going to school, they closed the school down. They didn't want us to have an education." That was probably when she told me, "They can take anything from you, but they can't take what's in your head." And that was something that really kind of resonated with me. She said, "Unless they knock you over the head and you get amnesia" (personal communication, March 7, 2022).

References

All-White academy loses tax exempt status. (1985, October 20). *Clarion-Ledger.* https://www.newspapers.com/article/clarion-ledger/140719797

Bonastia, C. (2012). *Southern stalemate: Five years without public education in Prince Edward County, Virginia.* The University of Chicago Press.

Britzman, D. P. (1998). *Lost subjects, contested objects: Toward a psychoanalytic inquiry of learning* (1st ed.). State University of New York Press.

Craig, J. (2010). Black resilience vs. White resistance in Prince Edward County. In T. Hicks & A. Pitre (Eds.), *The educational lockout of African Americans in Prince Edward County, Virginia (1959–1964): Personal accounts and reflections* (pp. 47–54). University Press of America.

Dayton-Wood, A., Hammonds, L., Matherson, L., & Tollison, L. (2012). Bridging gaps and preserving memories through oral history research and writing. *English Journal, 101*(4), 77–82.

Drake, W. (1979). Tax status of private segregated schools: The new revenue procedure. *William & Mary Law Review, 20*(3). https://scholarship.law.wm.edu/wmlr/vol20/iss3/4

Dunn, R. S. (2022). *Popular memory, silence, and trust: A mother and son's relationship to school in the shadow of the Prince Edward County closures.* [Master's thesis]. University of Massachusetts Boston.

Dutt-Doner, K. M., Allen, S., & Campanaro, K. (2016). Understanding the impact of using oral histories in the classroom. *The Social Studies, 107*(6), 257–265. https://doi.org/10.1080/00377996.2016.1221792

Ellsworth, S. (1982). *Death in a promised land: The Tulsa race riot of 1921.* Louisiana State University Press.

Foner, E. (1998). *The story of American freedom* (1st ed.). W. W. Norton.

Foner, E. (2015). The story of American freedom—Before and after 9/11. In *Contested democracy* (pp. 301–312). Columbia University Press. https://doi.org/10.7312/sinh14110-015

Garrett, H. J. (2017). *Learning to be in the world with others: Difficult knowledge & social studies education.* Peter Lang.

Green, R. L., & Hoffmann, L. J. (1965). A case study of the effects of educational deprivation on southern rural Negro children. *The Journal of Negro Education, 34*(3), 327–341.

Green, R. L., & Morgan, R. F. (1969). The effects of resumed schooling on the measured intelligence of Prince Edward County's Black children. *The Journal of Negro Education, 38*(2), 147–155. https://doi.org/10.2307/2294274

Gross, M. H., & Terra, L. (Eds.). (2018). *Teaching and learning the difficult past: Comparative perspectives* (1st ed.). Routledge.

Harris, L. M., Sheppard, M., & Levy, S. A. (2022). *Teaching difficult histories in difficult times: Stories of practice.* Teachers College Press.

Hoffman, E. (2004). *After such knowledge: Memory, history, and the legacy of the Holocaust.* Public Affairs.

Johnson, M. M., & Mason, P. B. (2017). "Just talking about life": Using oral histories of the Civil Rights Movement to encourage classroom dialogue on race. *Teaching Sociology, 45*(3), 279–289. https://doi.org/10.1177/0092055X17690431

Kyriakoudes, L. (2023, December 18). *Information about IRBs and oral history.* Oral History Association. https://oralhistory.org/information-about-irbs

Simon, R. I. (2014). *A pedagogy of witnessing: Curatorial practice and the pursuit of social justice* (1st ed.). State University of New York Press.

Stoddard, J. (2022). Difficult knowledge and history education. *Pedagogy, Culture & Society, 30*(3), 383–400. https://doi.org/10.1080/14681366.2021.1977982

Titus, J. O. (2011). *Brown's battleground: Students, segregationists, and the struggle for justice in Prince Edward County, Virginia.* University of North Carolina Press.

Trouillot, M.-R. (1995). *Silencing the past: Power and the production of history.* Beacon Press.

Williams, R. (2013). *How direct descendants of a school lockout achieved academic success: Resilience in the educational attainments of Prince Edward County's children.* PhD dissertation. William & Mary. Paper 1550154190. https://doi.org/10.25774/w4-jwpq-e185

Woodson, A. N. (2016). We're just ordinary people: Messianic master narratives and Black youths' civic agency. *Theory & Research in Social Education, 44*(2), 184–211. https://doi.org/10.1080/00933104.2016.1170645

Zembylas, M. (2014). Theorizing "difficult knowledge" in the aftermath of the "affective turn": Implications for curriculum and pedagogy in handling traumatic representations. *Curriculum Inquiry, 44*(3), 390–412. https://doi.org/10.1111/curi.12051

Additional Reading

Oral histories. (n.d.). UCLA Library | Center for Oral History Research. https://oralhistory.library.ucla.edu/pages/family_history

Appendix: Adapted Life History Questions

Childhood

A. Early Childhood/Initial Experiences Regarding Education

- What were/are your parents like?
- Where was your family originally from? Were they originally from Farmville, or did they make their way there?
- What stories did you hear growing up about your family, and their education?
- What were your parents' attitudes toward education before/after the school closures?
- Do you feel like you internalized any of their perceptions as a young student?
- What did your parents do for a living?
- As a child, did you contribute to the family income or help your parents in their work in any way?
- What was your parents' religious background?
- How was religion observed in your home?
- What were your parents' political beliefs?
- What political/other organizations were your parents involved in?
- What other relatives did you have contact with growing up?
- Describe your siblings and their interactions with you when you were young. What did you do together? What conflicts did you have?
- What were your family's economic circumstances? Do you remember any times when money was tight? Do you remember having to do without things they wanted or needed?
- What were your duties around the house as a child?
- What skills did you learn (e.g., cooking, carpentry, crafts) and who taught them? What activities did the family do together?

B. Community

- Describe the community you grew up in and especially your own neighborhood.
- Can you remember the races and ethnicities in your neighborhood?
- What did people do for a living?
- Were there notable class differences?
- Where did people shop?
- What was the largest town or city they remember visiting when they were young and what were your impressions of it?

C. Early Schooling

- Describe your school friend, or your favorite teachers (if you had any). Were there any mentors that inspired you or moments that strained your relationship with education?
- Did you have any favorite subjects?
- Were there any special activities at either school that have struck you?
- Were there moments where you felt especially alienated/homesick? Can you tell me about them?
- Were there any moments where you experienced discipline from figures in power? What did this look/feel like?
- Did you experience any teasing or bullying at school?

D. Friends and Interests

- What did you do in your spare time after school?
- Who were your friends and what did you do when you got together?
- What were your plans when you finished school? Education? Work?
- What did you want to be when you grew up?
- Were there different groups in school? Which did you belong to? How do you think you were perceived by others?

E. Work

- Did you work any jobs during your teenage years or at school?
- Were you contributing to the family income? If not, how did you spend money?

Adulthood

F. Further Education

- Can you describe your relationship to higher education? Did you go to school for more degrees? What drove this desire/was there a goal in mind?
- Did you reflect upon your earlier experiences in education as you worked to get your advanced degree?

G. Adult Work

- How did your childhood perspectives on education and society influence your adult working life?

H. Marriage or Formation of Significant Relationships

- How did you meet? What drew you together?
- Describe your decision to marry/move in together.
- Did you talk about your experience with the education system to your significant other? What was their reaction?
- What was most difficult being in a relationship originally? What was most satisfying?
- Were there any significant changes in your relationship?

I. Children

- What were/are your children like when they were/are young. How have they changed or not changed?
- What was your relationship with your children like when they were young versus your relationship with them now?
- What activities did your family do together?
- Do you have any established family traditions?
- What was most satisfying to you about raising children? What was most difficult?
- What values do you try to raise your children with? How did you go about doing that?

CHAPTER 7

SCHOOL HAS A "PLACE" … EVERY PLACE EXCEPT FARMVILLE, PRINCE EDWARD COUNTY, VIRGINIA

Alicia Pennington
Temple University, USA

The only thing I ever thought about was I wanted to get the best education that I could. —Edwilda Issac (Miles-Turner, 2004)

Introduction

As we approach the possible unraveling of democracy in 2024 America, it is important to focus on the issues that surround access to a quality education as a civil and moral right. While attempts to rewrite the impacts of the American education system are consciously, systematically, and determinedly gaining momentum in our present, it is important to critique how the education landscape was shaped by events in our past. It is vital to crystalize how particular segments of the American population viewed education as a foundational underpinning of democracy. When that "place" of education is systematically undermined, that "place" becomes a study environment.

In 1848, when Horace Mann posited that education was the great equalizer (Cremin, 1964), he could not have foreseen how the myriad of education landscapes would shift so dramatically and become the seats of public and private contestations. From school rooms to school boards, from high school walkouts to college protests, to the resegregation of classrooms and buildings, the education landscapes have been maneuvered to shift dramatically and purposefully toward reinforcing divisions in the existing reproduction of social classes. One of the salient issues that pushed an existing, self-serving, functioning—albeit segregated—education structure to the breaking point was the unequal school constructs in Farmville, Virginia.

For nearly four centuries, learning in spite of opposition "has been a recurring theme in the educational history of African Americans" (Span, 2005, p. 26). From its inception in colonial Virginia, education has had different actors, a variety of motivations, and uneven outcomes for African Americans. The Bray School in 18th-century Williamsburg, Virginia, operated from 1760 to 1774 (McClain, 2012; Roos, 2022) and educated approximately 400 of both the free and enslaved. However, by the 20th century, Virginia's education went from colonial access to a complete county shutdown. Despite the ebb and flow of interactions across the geographic education landscape, whether it was in the colonial era, during and after enslavement, or in the 20th century, African Americans have consistently envisioned access to public education not only as a civil, human, and moral right but also as the vehicle of mobility and the embodiment of unlimited possibilities. The "place" of education was no less important.

W. E. B. Du Bois (1898)[1] in his study of Negroes in Farmville, Virginia, maintained that because Prince Edward County had no school for its colored children, it was necessary to send them outside county limits (disrupting their sense of "place"). What this early study revealed was that the education landscape, already fractured by race, was softened for dissent. By the mid-20th century, galvanized African Americans began to demand equality and inclusion in the education processes, particularly regarding their full participation as citizens (Cochran, 2021).

Depending on the drivers of any movement, not only has a gap existed in the quest for education parity, but also the education landscape itself had veered away from even a pretense of its "separate but equal" comparison. The importance of "place" would redefine the existing contours of why, how, and who delivered the purposeful and concentrated education inequalities across the geographic landscape.

By mid-century America, a group of young activists would be called to action. On April 23, 1951, 16-year-old high school student Barbara Johns organized an unprecedented school walkout of 450 students from the Robert Russa Moton[2] High School in the small town of Farmville, Virginia. Kluger (1976) recounted the clarity of Ms. Johns's issues with clear objectives:

It was time that Negroes were treated equally with whites. It was time that they had a decent high school. They were going to march out of school then and there and they were going to stay out until the white community responded properly (p. 468).

Ms. Johns may not have been aware that she sat at the nexus of three extraordinary education movements. The first was the initial 86-year (1865–1951) period following the Civil War. According to Williams (2002), during enslavement, the very act of learning to read had been a form of liberation and resistance, but now it became one of life's necessities. Years of enslavement planted the seeds of determination for education. The newly freed Blacks[3] understood the importance of education in the lives of their children and were now able to realize education as a certainty. This thirst for schooling, according to Anderson (1988), was actualized in the consistent contributions of the previously enslaved who would provide what few pennies they had toward their children's education.

Ms. Johns, niece of the civil rights pioneer the Rev. Vernon Johns, boldly stepped into this activist space and led her fellow students to protest the conditions at the Robert Russa Moton High School. Years later, Ms. Johns recounted that the student protesters in 1951 understood that their movement not only resonated in Farmville but also "would broadcast Prince Edward County around the world" (Olson, 2001, p. 81).

The second movement, the 1951 school protest, which some scholars have contended was the beginning of the modern civil rights era (Hohl, 1993; Miles-Turner, 2004; Sitkoff, 1981), was the first in a series of what later would be chronicled as the student-led civil rights movement. These later movements, initiated in the 1960s with lunch-counter boycotts in North Carolina, were informed by college students, while Farmville, Virginia, was led by high schoolers.

The third event was the impact of the 1954 Supreme Court decision in *Brown vs Board of Education*. The original court case, *Davis v. County School Board of Prince Edward County*, that arose from the strike was one of the five cases decided by the Court and was the only case initiated by students. According to Rothstein (2014), the *Brown* decision annihilated the "separate but equal" *Plessy v. Ferguson* decision, sanctioned by the Supreme Court in 1896. *Plessy* permitted states to define schools as "Whites only" and "Negroes only." This student crusade in Farmville in their positionality for equal rights in education drew Martin Luther King Jr. and other national leaders to visit the area. Today, the Robert Russa Moton High School, the site of the 1951 student strike, is a National Historic Landmark, a civil rights museum, and the centerpiece of Virginia's Civil Rights in Education Heritage Trail. It honors the efforts of local students and citizens who paved the way for integrated public education nationwide.

One of the most important aspects of the student protest in Farmville, and the subsequent closing of schools, was the recognition of the importance of "place" in focusing the nation's attention on the egregious disparities in the delivery of education. This attention later inspired a wave of future freedom riders, sit-ins, voter registration efforts, and other acts of resistance that would culminate in civil rights legislation in the late 1950s and 1960s.

Literature Review

Geographies of Education

The landscapes for research in the field of geographies of education varied widely. The growing importance of this field was recognized by two journals through special editions. While the subdiscipline has not isolated the concept of "place" as it relates to this paper, it has segregated other areas for study. *Geographical Research* (2017), and *Urban Studies* (2007) each devoted a special edition of essays covering various aspects of the geographies of education. These editions articulated a variety of *subdisciplinary* lenses in human geography, including political, urban, social, and cultural geographies with the potentiality for expansive research.

Because of the vastness of research areas, the literature review had a limited conceptual framework (1) to make note of the development and different perspectives in the geographies of education and (2) to examine the geographies of education from the standpoint of the importance of "place" in the education processes in Farmville, Virginia, across disciplines. "Place" for this paper relies on Relph's (1976) limited definition describing *place* as an appreciation of a place's character, individuality, and uniqueness. Rogers et al. (2013) in the *Dictionary of Human Geography* reinforced this concept, arguing that attention should also be paid to how people value and interpret the places they inhabit in the present or have inhabited in the past. "Place," therefore, has a dual identity as represented by the school building and as where education life happens.

As we excavate the range of research in the areas of the geographies of education, several scholars have outlined distinct interests. Among these are Kraftl et al. (2022), who called for "cross-fertilization" of the subdiscipline; Oswin (2020), who engaged the concepts of marginalized communities; and Alderman et al. (2022), who focused on nonformal education spaces. It is also important to note that much of the early scholarship in this (sub) discipline identified analytic perspectives in an array of connective areas. Foci have ranged from a concentration on spaces of formal education and learning (Nicholson, 2023) to those that examine geographies from the vantages of identities, inequalities, and political transformations (Collins & Coleman, 2008).

Thiem (2008) drew our attention to the geographies of education quickening in pace, volume, and reach while increasingly the importance of work being "strategically decentered and outward-looking" and "deliberately situates its object(s) of analysis relative to broader research programs" (p. 155).

However, Manzo and Devine-Wright's (2021) literature reviews on "place" and place-based concepts (e.g., attachment, identity, satisfaction, and dependence) have developed no consensus on theory, methods, and application to investigate these concepts.

There are additional areas that have also expanded the parameters of the discipline by analyzing social and spatial exclusions, neoliberal economic restructuring, the relationships between education and spatial inequalities, social mobilities and education, privatization, education as generative, and the importance of education's poststructuralist dimensions (Kraftl, 2013; Nicholson, 2023). Brock (2016) set a wider scope for this interdisciplinary field, maintaining there are essential affinities between geography and education studies that emphasize education systems and other forms of knowledge transfer.

Adjacent to the geographies of education is another emerging geographic investigative platform: Black geographies. Harris and Hyden (2017) argued that because both geographies are relatively new landscapes of investigation, they open vibrant lanes for reimagining and understanding racialized productions of spaces. In looking at the school closing in Farmville through a geographic lens and understanding the importance of "place" in the "Black belt,"[4] this issue is at the crossroads of geographies of education. It then becomes possible to see that it fits neatly into several areas of this rapidly solidifying field of geography. The literature in this emerging area of geographic studies is at the intersectionality of the social sciences. The notions of "place" are symbols in sociology, history, and political science and cover vast areas of geography. By examining "place" through a geographical lens from the social sciences, there is an enhanced capacity to contribute an even deeper understanding of the multifaceted nature of education.

The Importance of "Place"

As the formerly enslaved moved cautiously toward freedom, two ideals of place became fused in importance. First, one of the most fundamentally precious places in the Black community became the "place" where education happened: the school. Thiem (2008) concurred, adding that historically Black education spaces have generally produced distinctive spatial and ideological expressions of nonformal education.

Second, Anderson (1988) asserts that education was so important that "ex-slaves were first among native southerners to wage a campaign for universal public education" (p. 18). He underscored that freed people would not only build their schools but also recruit teachers from whoever was literate in their community. He also highlighted the notion of place and its valuable influences in education spaces. He maintained that children who remained in their geographic "place" "would walk miles on unpaved roads to schools in order to gain a fair education" (p. 237).

Weber (2001) further illuminated the importance of "place" both as a structure and as an emotional center by identifying the deliverables of education as promoters of cultural beliefs and as places of initial socialization. Schools and the education processes that happen within their walls are two of the things most of us have in common. Consequently, in 1959 when schools closed in Farmville, Virginia, this "place" ceased to be a site of community cohesion around education. Instead, parents, friends, students, religious leaders, and politicians became community allies and advocates in continuing the cooperative nature of school and education as the place where personal and private histories were written and rewritten. Nguyen et al. (2017) contended that actions like school closings, and their responses, demand geographic attention to the confluence of schooling arrangements.

Education in the African American community historically has been viewed as a precursor to social mobility. Many of the corridors in US society, however, have been driven by the inclusion or exclusion of specific groups of students from school. Because school has traditionally been the key access point to social mobility, it has also been a site of major conflict. When schools closed in 1959 as a response to the landmark 1954 Supreme Court *Brown v. Board* decision,[5] access to formal education for Farmville's Black children—housed in inadequate facilities, staffed by underpaid teachers, and with outdated materials—nevertheless came to an end for nearly 1,400 school-age children.

The impacts of the denial of access to education in the lives of Farmvillians was noted by Shaw (1996), who elevated our understanding of the duality and importance of place and education. Writing that communities organized around the concept of "place" and education are locations that believe children "completing their education, in addition to serving as good examples of the consequences of individual effort, ambition, and ability … represents one of the best traditions of the community" (p. 67). Consequently, schools as "place," as geographic sites, have parameters that expand not only children's knowledge and behaviors but also their identities.

Against the historical backdrop of anti-literacy laws from 1740 to the 1840s, from Virginia to Louisiana (Maddox, 2022), the desire for an education never wavered in the Black community.

The challenges presented by the Farmville school closings opened an education chasm that would be partially filled by an extraordinary group of individuals supporting Black families in finding alternatives to educate their children.

Initially, families in Prince Edward County would scramble to educate their children on their own. Some residents were able to arrange for their children to live with family and friends outside Prince Edward County and could enroll them in local schools. Others were given the opportunity to continue their children's education through outside agencies. Through the leadership of two ministers—Reverend L. Francis Griffin (Baptist) and Reverend A. I. Dunlap (African Methodist Episcopal)—arrangements for some of the students were made with Kittrell Junior College, a historically African American junior college (closed in 1975); the Southern Interagency Council; the American Friends Service Committee; the National Association for the Advancement of Colored People; community leaders; and teachers' unions. All of these agents coordinated to find host families and facilities available to educate many of the locked-out children (Lowe, 2010). Despite these herculean efforts, for all Farmville children—whether educated in a church, at home, or in an unfamiliar county or city—their physical, biographical, and geographical sense of the "place" was disrupted.

The review underscores that the need for "place," much like previously mentioned areas of research, should be a stand-alone platform. The ground has been seeded for continued examination of "place" as an isolated area for research. Scannell and Gifford (2010) proposed a person-process-place model to explain meanings attached to places in a "comprehensive" and "structured" manner. Manzo and Perkins (2006) have developed a model to accommodate people-place relations in community participation and planning by which place meaning and attachment play pivotal roles across processes.

Efforts are being made across the American landscape to physically, emotionally, psychologically, and educationally reframe access. However, according to Healey (2005) and Stephenson (2010), at this juncture it is critical to remind ourselves that people shape their places, and places reshape their inhabitants. In examining the lives of the Black families in Farmville, Virginia, we become witnesses to both.

Methodology

The research in the field of geographies of education has expanded across disciplines. From economics to sociology to political science, the field is complex and diverse. Several scholars have engaged the breadth of research, with Waters (2016) drawing attention to both the quantity and scope of research in this subdiscipline, while Puttick (2022) added that this expansion includes generative synergies across multiple diverse areas of research.

To present a qualitatively narrow, restrictive, and nuanced methodological approach to the concept of "place" in this field, I initially designed a series of applicable search keywords, descriptors, concepts, and Boolean logic to search Education Resources Information Center. Often the Boolean searches do not identify all the relevant literature and frequently capture books and articles only tangentially relevant. I also used Google Scholar with the same search terms. To conduct an even more extensive search, I examined the descriptor and keywords associated with each article and conducted additional searches.

Over 112 books and articles published from 1990 to 2022 were generated. Because the search terms were broad, it was possible to then scan authors, titles, and abstracts and add several more terms—such as "education and place," "education in Virginia," and "place as a notion"—generating additional articles from 2010 to 2023. After each search, I eliminated results outside my research area. Because subject terms are invariably different across databases, I amassed a collection of relevant keyword terms that could potentially locate "place" as a geographic concept in those databases for future research.

It cannot be overstated that the research for this paper was developed to present an amalgamation of views on the importance of "place" in a community that was under education siege. Bonastia (2012) pointed out the commitment to "place" in the lives of the residents of Farmville. He argued that the Prince Edward County story stands as a "critical chapter … an example … of black perseverance from the 1951 student strike to the 1964 reopening of schools" (p. 161). This could only have been accomplished through their allegiance to "place."

Using a geographic lens to coordinate information on the notion of "place" as a unifying concept allows the geographies of education to come into clearer focus. Using literature across disciplines to guide us through this subdiscipline provides an additional long-term and overarching benefit. Because this chapter is rooted in a historical time frame, the rationale for using the broad conceptual frameworks from the social sciences made it possible to produce extensive articles for review. Their exposure increases the capacity to fill research gaps in the geographies of education.

Results and Discussion

When I began research into the importance of "place" in the lives of the residents of Farmville, Virginia, through the geographies-of-education lens, I expected to find numerous journal articles. Instead, I found only a few that were directly connected to "place" as I defined it. My concentration necessarily shifted from a straight geographic line to a circuitous drive through adjacent social sciences. This was both revelatory and expansive.

It's important in this section to note two unexpected discoveries in the data search. The first was the forecasts for a possible new challenge for the geographies of education. Kraftl et al. (2022) pointed to Gough et al.

(2019), who determined that the field "needs to consider what equitable inclusion scholarship in geographies of education might look like, and to find ways to decolonize the scholarship in ways to decenter these approaches that currently predominate" (p. 20).

The second observation was alerting researchers to a name change. What had been the "Higher Education Research Group" was now the "Geography and Education Research Group" (Kraftl et al., 2022). This platform change began by providing contemporary researchers with the historical roots and language traditions of the geographies of education. It delineated the different subdisciplinary areas that research on geographies of education has contributed, including social reproduction, mobilities, the relationship between education spaces and learner agency, cyber learners, structural inequalities, and materialities.

Geographies of education is attempting to identify educational processes across time and space. From opportunity to outcome, from a geographical perspective, it contextualizes that there are differential and relational disparate consequences for individuals and groups. In this environment, an analysis of the school closings in Farmville, Virginia, in 1959 made it possible to isolate and redefine the importance of "place" and uncover both the intensity and complex nature of attachment.

This "place"—Farmville, Virginia—and its African American residents—both children and adults—were rooted on a landscape divided by race, access, and education. The attention drawn to the decision to close schools, to prevent integration, could only be underscored by the reaction of the Department of Justice through the attorney general.

In a speech to honor the centennial of the Emancipation Proclamation[6] in 1963, Robert F. Kennedy spoke of the school closings, telling attendees:

> We must achieve equal education opportunities for all our children regardless of race. Segregated schools cause educational as well as psychological difficulties and the resulting drain on our greatest resource—the spirit and knowledge of our children—must be eliminated. We may observe, with as much sadness as irony that outside of Africa, south of the Sahara where education is still a difficult challenge, the only places on earth known not to provide free public education are Communist China, North Vietnam, Sarawak, Singapore, British Honduras—*and Prince Edward County, Virginia* (italics added).

In Farmville, Virginia, the 1950s was a decade shadowed by events. It began with students' dissatisfaction with the conditions at Robert Russa Moton High School, then the possibility of change with *Brown v. Board*, and ultimately the unimaginable threats of school closings. When schools *did* close in 1959, the continuity of community, family, and education was disrupted in their most sacred "place."

Implications for Practice and Research

In the review of literature for this paper, it came into focus that there is an area to research independently the interrelationships between education, community, and "place." Also, two critical investigative avenues were opened by Steadman et al. (2006), who maintained that "place" can be understood individually and imagined collectively. The individual and collective shapes made by the residents of Farmville, Virginia, through history, family, religion, and education were transformed by the school closings. The 1959 shutting of all school buildings in Farmville and the deprivation of education allowed one community to preserve their "place," while altering the education and "place" landscapes of another. As the examination of "place" broadens, other crucial elements in its importance surface. Symbolic meanings and attachments (evident in the honoring of Moton High School[7]), identifiable behaviors, and the construction of identities are moored in a sense of "place." The explorative landscapes created by the geographies of education have expanded greatly. The wide lanes of explorative research have expanded outward. Erfani (2022) maintained that this outward reach has the potential to capture analysis of feminist, Afrocentric, social network, autonomist, and other critical traditions that can influence cultural and political geographies.

Moving forward, researchers studying place will expand and refine how we conceptualize the concepts and notions of the individual and collective understanding of "place." The study of "place" implies more than a singular, cohesive view. When "place" is connected to an issue like education, it requires two standpoints. In Farmville, Virginia, in 1959, "place" not only (a) represented the physical structures on the landscape but also (b) became irrevocably linked to education. Comprehensive and structured research has the potential to excavate conceptual understandings of how "place" and the communities it holds continue to survive when they are under relentless assault.

Conclusion

This chapter investigated—across the social sciences—articles and a small number of books regarding the importance of "place" in the education lives of the Black community. The focus and concentration then narrowed to one community: Farmville, Virginia, from 1951 to 1964. In prioritizing the informational cache, the accumulated materials provided an overview of scholarship through a geographic lens on how allegiance to "place" influences a community's relationship to education.

As a caveat, it is important to note here that according to Erfani (2022), scholars and the social sciences disciplines have viewed "place" differently, and they "have long attempted to frame these complex relations and interdependencies in a theoretical domain. There are a variety of models and conceptual frameworks developed to map out the relationships between people and their places" (p. 452).

When the children of Farmville were "locked out" of the school building, education was not their only loss. The importance of the school building itself and its bearing on the educational and geographic landscapes cannot be overlooked. The school closings, the inability to access the buildings, and the education within presented this "place" with a dizzying, unparalleled, severing of community consistencies.

America in the 1950s was presented with a challenge to remedy the cascading and widespread damages woven across and into the lives of its African American citizenry. *Plessy v. Ferguson*,[8] was designed to restrict access to public accommodations. The May 17, 1954, *Brown v. Board* decision was to address this "separate but equal" doctrine that allowed the segregation of school systems across the landscapes of the United States.

In Farmville, the *Brown v. Board* decision exacerbated a southern education system already primed to decimate the education and attachment to "place" in the lives of 1,400 Black children. This notion of "place" sat at the foundational interconnections of education, memory, security, community and individual interaction, and identity. Each of these areas would experience decades of disruption in the lives of the residents of Prince Edward County.

Finally, Leslie Fenwick made one of the most convincing ancillary discussions delineating several of the ripple effects of school closings not only in Farmville but also across segregated school systems. In *Jim Crow's Pink Slip* (2022), Fenwick provided a cogent account of the long-term effects of the failure to integrate Black principals and teachers into desegregating schools, asserting it remains the unfulfilled promise of *Brown*. These failures were consciously promoted, encouraged, and maintained to guarantee the segregationists' control over school systems.

Fenwick (2022) continued by drawing connections from past injustices to contestations that educational systems contend with today, including, but not limited to, underrepresentation of Black teachers and principals, systemic inequalities, differentials in salary and salary reductions, and finally, teacher shortages. Connecting "place" to these lingering issues further illuminates the tragedy of the unrealized American democratic ideals of an integrated society with equal access to educational opportunities. When schools closed in 1959, in Farmville, Virginia, the message received in that community was clear: Their children's education aspirations were of no value.

Notes

1. Du Bois's study was the first social science study of the Negro.
2. The school was named for Robert Russa Moton, one of the most prominent Black educators in the United States in the first decades of the 20th century.

The original high school was built in 1939 for 100 students and was augmented later with buildings made from plywood and tar paper, with no plumbing or heating to house over 400 students (Heinemann, 2020).
3. *Blacks* and *African Americans* are used interchangeably to identify persons of African descent. Negroes is used in its historical context.
4. The "Black Belt" was described by sociologist Arthur Raper (1930) as follows:

> In the heart of the South, there are approximately 200 counties in which over half the population is Negro. These counties are like a crescent from Virginia to Texas and constitute the Black Belt.... The Black Belt includes the most fertile soil of the South (3).

As a Black geographical space, the Black Belt South has been subjected to the commissions and omissions of state and federal policies, illuminating that "black and poor subjects are disposable precisely because they cannot easily move or escape" (McKittrick & Woods, 2007, p. 3). However, the deep, rich history of counter-movements and mobilizations include slave uprisings, the Underground Railroad, biracial populist farmers movements, and the 1960s Civil Rights Movement. The Black Belt is also, according to Harris and Hyden (2017), "home to 34% of the nation's population living in poverty" (p. 53).

5. The original court case, *Davis v. County School Board of Prince Edward County*, that arose from the strike was one of the five cases decided by the Supreme Court.
6. Delivered at Freedom Hall, Louisville, Kentucky, March 18, 1963.
7. On August 31, 1998, Robert Russa Moton High School achieved a National Historic Landmark designation for its significance to the *Brown v. Board of Education* US Supreme Court case.
8. *Plessy v. Ferguson* was a landmark 1896 US Supreme Court decision that upheld the constitutionality of racial segregation under the "separate but equal" doctrine. As a result, restrictive Jim Crow legislation and separate public accommodations based on race became commonplace.

References

Alderman, D. H., Craig, B., Inwood, F. J., & Cunningham, S. (2022). The 1964 freedom schools as neglected chapter in geography. *Journal of Geography in Higher Education, 47*(3), 411–431.

Anderson, J. W. (1988). *The education of Blacks in the South, 1860–1935*. University of North Carolina Press.

Bonastia, C. (2012). *Southern stalemate*. University of Chicago Press.

Brock, C. (2016). *Geography of education: Scale, space, and location in the study of education*. Bloomsbury Academic.

Butler, T., & Hamnett, C. (2007). The geography of education: Introduction. *Urban Studies, 44*(7), 1161–1174.

Cochran, E. (2021). *It seemed like reaching for the moon, southside Virginia's civil rights struggle against the Virginia way: 1951–1964*. PhD dissertation. University of South Carolina.

Collins, D., & Coleman, T. (2008). Social geographies of education: Looking within, and beyond, school boundaries. *Geography Compass, 2*(1), 281–299.

L. A. Cremin, (Ed.). (1964), *The transformation of the school and progressivism in American education, 1876–1957.* Random House.

Du Bois, W. E. B. (1898). The Negroes in Farmville, Virginia: A social study. *Bulletin of U. S. Bureau of Labor, 14,* 1–38.

Erfani, G. (2022). Reconceptualizing sense of place: Towards a conceptual framework for investigating individual-community-place relationships. *Journal of Planning Literature, 31*(3), 452–466.

Fenwick, L. (2022). *Jim Crow's pink slip.* Harvard University Press.

Gough, K. V., Langevang, T., Yankson, P. W. K., & Owusu, G. (2019). Shaping geographies of informal education: A global south perspective. *Annals of the American Association of Geographers, 109*(6), 1885–1902.

Harris, R., & Hyden, H. (2017). Special edition: Black geographies in and of the United States South. Geographies of resistance within the Black Belt South. *Southeastern Geographer, 57*(1), 51–61.

Healey, P. (2005). Editorial. *Planning Theory, 6*(11), 5–8.

Heinemann, R. (2020, December 7). Moton School Strike and Prince Edward County School Closings. In *Encyclopedia Virginia.* https://encyclopediavirginia.org/entries/moton-school-strike-and-prince-edward-county-school-closings

Hohl, L. A. (1993). *Open the doors: An analysis of Prince Edward County, Virginia Free School Association.* MA thesis. The University of Richmond.

Kluger, R. (1976). *Simple justice: The history of Brown v. Board of Education and Black struggle for equality.* Alfred Knopf.

Kraftl, P. (2013). Beyond 'voice,' beyond 'agency,' 'politics'? Hybrid childhood and some critical reflections on children's emotional geographies. *Emotion, Space and Society, 9,* 13–23.

Kraftl, P., Andrews, W., Beech, S., Ceresa, G., Holloway, S., Johnson, V., & White, C. (2022). Geographies of education: A journey. *Area, 54,* 15–23.

Lowe, J. (2010). *Prince Edward County, Virginia school closings.* Virginia Commonwealth Social Welfare History Project.

Maddox, C. (2022). *Literacy by any means necessary: The history of anti-literacy laws in the United States.* https://oaklandliteracycoalition.org/literacy-by-any-means-necessary-the-history-of-anti-literacy-laws-in-the-us

Manzo, L. C., & Devine-Wright, P. (2021). *Place attachment: Advances in theory, methods and applications* (2nd ed.). Routledge Press.

Manzo, L. C., & Perkins, D. D. (2006). Finding common ground: The importance of place attachment to community participation and planning. *Journal of Planning Literature, 20*(4), 335–350.

McClain, J. (2012). Archaeologists seek evidence of 18th century Bray School. *William & Mary News Archive.*

McKittrick, K., & Woods, C. (Eds.). (2007), *Black geographies and the politics of place.* South End Press.

Miles-Turner, K. (2004). Both victor and victim: Prince Edward County, Virginia, the NAACP and "Brown.". *Virginia Law Review.*

Nguyen, N., Cohen, D., & Huff, A. (2017). Catching the bus: A call for critical geographies of education. *Geography Compass, 11*(8), 1–13.

Nicholson, J. F. (2023). Historical geographies of alternative, and non-formal education: Learning from the histories of Black education. *Geography Compass, 17*(11), 1–13.
Olson, J. (2001). *Freedom's a daughters*. Scribner.
Oswin, N. (2020). An other geography. *Dialogues in Human Geography, 10*(1), 9–18.
Pini, B., Gulson, K. N., Kraftl, P., & Dufty-Jones, R. (2017). Critical geographies of education: An introduction. *Geographical Research, 55*(1), 13–17.
Puttick, S. (2022). Geographical education 1: Fields interactions and relationships. *Progress in Human Geography, 36*(3), 898–890.
Raper, A. (1930). *Preface to peasantry: A tale of two Black belt counties*. University of North Carolina Press.
Relph, E. C. (1976). *Place and powerlessness*. Pion Press.
Rogers, A., Castree, N., & Kitchin, R. (2013). *A dictionary of human geography*. Oxford University Press.
Roos, D. (2022). What school was like in the 13 colonies. https://www.history.com/news/13-colonies-school
Rothstein, R. (2014). *Brown v. Board at 60: Why have we been so disappointed? What have we learned?* Economic Policy Institute.
Scannell, L., & Gifford, R. (2010). Defining place attachment: A tripartite organizing framework. *Journal of Environmental Psychology, 30*(1), 1–10.
Shaw, S. J. (1996). *What woman ought to be and to do*. University of Chicago Press.
Sitkoff, H. (1981). *The struggle for Black equality, 1954–1980*. Hill and Wang.
Span, C. M. (2005). Learning in spite of opposition: African Americans and their history of educational exclusion in antebellum America. *Counterpoints, 131*, 26–53.
Steadman, R., Amsden, B. L., & Kruger, L. (2006). Sense of place and community: Points of intersection with implications for leisure research. *Leisure/Loisir, 30*(2), 393–404.
Stephenson, J. (2010). People and place. *Planning Theory and Practice, 11*(1), 9–21.
Thiem, H. C. (2008). Thinking through education: The geographies of contemporary educational restructuring. *Progress in Human Geography, 33*(2), 154–173.
Waters, H. (2016). Education unbound? Enlivening debates with a mobilities perspective on learning. *Progress in Human Geography, 41*(3), 270–298.
Weber, L. (2001). *Understanding race, class, gender, and sexuality*. McGraw Hill.
Williams, H. A. (2002). Clothing themselves in intelligence: The freedpeople, schooling, and northern teachers, 1861–1871. *Perspectives on African American Educational History, 87*, 372–389.

INDEX

14th Amendment, 28, 30, 36, 43, 78

academic achievement, 93
Allen v. County School Board of Prince Edward County, 39–40

the Black Belt, 31, 133, 140n4
Bolling v. Sharpe, 29
Briggs v. Elliott, 29
Brown II, 38, 72, 80
Brown Scholarship Fund, xix–xx, 1, 3–17
Brown v. Board of Education, xvii, xix–xx, 3, 14, 22, 24, 27, 29, 50, 52–53, 71, 80, 89, 91, 140n7
Byrd, Harry, 23–24, 26, 30, 34–37, 41, 44n1, 112

case study, xviii–xx, 1, 4–5, 10, 71–72, 83, 89, 93–100, 103, 106–7, 114
Civil Rights Movement, xx, 3, 5, 22–27, 40–41, 44, 49–50, 54–55, 59–60, 64, 71–75, 77, 79, 82–83, 86, 97, 100, 113–15, 122, 131–32, 140n4
community, xvii, xx, 2–6, 8–17, 23, 27–28, 35, 38, 40–43, 50–51, 53–56, 58–60, 62–64, 66n12, 74, 76, 81, 89–90, 92–93, 95–96, 98, 100, 106–8, 112–18, 121–22, 126, 131–39
critical race theory (CRT), 3, 10, 91–92; critical race praxis, 4

Davis v. County School Board of Prince Edward County, xvii, 2–3, 27–29, 53, 65n3, 76, 79–80, 131, 140n5
difficult history, xx, 111, 115, 119–123. *See also* difficult knowledge
difficult knowledge, xx, 111, 115, 118–119. *See also* difficult history
direct action, 25, 44, 52, 74–75
Du Bois, W. E. B., xviii, 130, 139n1

education, xvii–xxi, 1–5, 7, 9, 11, 13–17, 21, 27–31, 33–35, 39, 41–43, 49–54, 57, 60–62, 64, 65n1, 66n11, 71–78, 81–86, 89–108, 112–15, 118–21, 123, 125–27, 129–39, 139–40n2; lost educational opportunity, 104–6. *See also* public school closures

143

144 Index

Farmville Herald, 31, 38, 42, 58, 79–80, 95. *See also* Farmville, Virginia

Farmville, Virginia, xviii, xxi, 6, 9, 24–25, 27, 31, 38, 40–42, 56, 59–60, 65nn8–9, 79, 82, 90, 100–2, 104–5, 125, 129–39. *See also* public school closures; Virginia (VA)

Gebhart v. Belton, 29

geographies of education, xx–xxi, 132–33, 135–39. *See also* importance of "place"

grassroots schools, xviii, 43. *See also* training centers

Griffen, Francis L., Rev., xviii, 27–28, 42–43, 54–55, 120, 135

Griffin v. School Board of Prince Edward County, 2, 43, 54, 76, 83

historic preservation, 3, 5, 50–51, 55, 57–60, 62–64

importance of "place," 130, 132–34, 136–38. *See also* geographies of education

Jim Crow, 22, 27, 30, 73, 77–78, 140n8; laws, 78, 140n8

Kilpatrick, James J., 23, 34, 36, 40
King, Martin Luther, Jr., Rev., xvii–xviii, 71–72, 75, 83, 113, 131

literacy exclusion, 10–11
lived experience, 4–5, 78, 95, 113–15, 118,
Lost Generation, 53, 55, 64, 80, 82

Marshall, Thurgood, 29–30, 71
massive resistance, xvii–xviii, xx, 22, 24–25, 30–31, 33–34, 36–37, 39, 42, 44n1, 50–51, 53–54, 58–61, 64, 65nn6–7, 72–73, 80, 90–91, 98, 112–14, 118. *See also Brown v. Board of Education*; Civil Rights Movement; Virginia (VA)

memory, xx, 22, 26, 33, 49–51, 54–55, 59, 61, 63–65, 65n2, 116, 119, 139. *See also* historic preservation

Moton High School. *See* Robert Russa Moton High School

National Association for the Advancement of Colored People (NAACP), 23–25, 27–33, 35, 37, 39, 41–43, 52–54, 64, 65n5, 72, 79, 83. *See also* Civil Rights Movement

oral history, xx, 114–16, 118, 121–123

Parks, Rosa, 71, 113
Plessy v. Ferguson, 30, 77–78, 131, 139, 140n8. *See also* "separate but equal"

primary source, xx, 72, 75–82, 85–86, 103, 116

Prince Edward County (PEC), Virginia, xvii–xxi, 1–5, 10–15, 21–29, 31–32, 37–44, 49–51, 53–64, 65n1, 65n3, 66n14, 71–86, 89–96, 98, 100–8, 111–15, 118, 120, 129–31, 135–37, 139, 140n5; microhistory of, xx, 72–73, 75, 85–86. *See also* Virginia (VA) public school closures, xvii–xxi, 2–5, 9–12, 14–15, 17, 22, 24, 26, 37, 39–43, 50–51, 53–55, 58, 60–64, 73–74, 76, 78, 81–85, 89–98, 100–8, 111–12, 114–16, 118, 120–21, 123, 125, 132–35, 137–39. *See also* education, lost educational opportunity

racial divide, 10, 12–14, 137
racial healing, xx, 14, 50–51, 60–63
racism, 3–4, 13, 15–16, 23, 51, 75, 92, 122
Reconstruction, 40, 76–78
redress, 1–4
restorative justice, xix–xx, 3–4, 10, 13–17
Robert Russa Moton High School, xviii, xx, 3, 5–6, 22, 27–30, 38, 49–65, 65n4, 65–66nn9–11, 72, 76, 79, 90, 101–2, 130–31, 137–38, 139–140n2, 140n7. *See also* Robert Russa Moton Museum
Robert Russa Moton Museum, 3, 5–6, 13, 50–51, 55, 59, 62–64, 77, 79, 81–82, 96–97, 102, 131. *See also* Robert Russa Moton High School

"separate but equal," 130–31, 139, 140n8. *See also Plessy v. Ferguson*
socialization, 33, 91–92, 134

social class, xviii, 22–23, 26, 92, 126, 130
school closings. *See* public school closures
school integration, xx, 1, 22–24, 26–27, 29, 31–32, 34–41, 43, 44n1, 50–51, 53, 60, 64, 72, 76, 80–81, 90, 95, 106, 112–13, 118–20, 131, 137, 139
silence, xx, 3, 12, 15, 24, 60, 115–17, 121–22
student: sit-in, 24, 43–44, 132; strike, xxi, 22–23, 27, 49, 52, 65n4, 79, 90, 131, 136, 140n5; walkout, 22, 27, 52, 76, 79, 130
Supreme Court, xvii, 1, 22, 26–27, 29–30, 32–33, 35–38, 40, 53–54, 59, 79–80, 90, 131, 134, 140n5, 140nn7–8. *See also* individual cases

training centers, 43. *See also* grassroots schools

Virginia (VA), xvii–xxi, 1–3, 5–8, 11, 13–17, 21–44, 44nn1–2, 49–50, 56–57, 59–60, 63, 65n1, 65n5, 65n8, 66n11, 66n16, 72–76, 78–84, 86, 89–90, 92, 94, 96–97, 102, 107–8, 112, 114, 130–32, 134–39, 140n4
Virginia Way, 22–23, 26, 30, 44, 73. *See also* Farmville, Virginia; Prince Edward County (PEC), Virginia

www.ingramcontent.com/pod-product-compliance
Lightning Source LLC
Chambersburg PA
CBHW050538300426
44113CB00012B/2165